McGraw-Hill's

500
Psychology
Questions

Also in McGraw-Hill's 500 Questions Series

McGraw-Hill's

500

Psychology
Questions

Ace Your College Exams

Kate C. Ledwith, DSW

New York Chicago San Francisco Lisbon London Madrid Mexico City
Milan New Delhi San Juan Seoul Singapore Sydney Toronto

ISBN   978-0-07-178036-0
MHID   0-07-178036-X

e-ISBN   978-0-07-178051-3
e-MHID   0-07-178051-3

Library of Congress Control Number 2011944609

McGraw-Hill products are available at special quantity discounts to use as premiums
and sales promotions or for use in corporate training programs. To contact a
representative, please e-mail us at bulksales@mcgraw-hill.com.

This book is printed on acid-free paper.

CONTENTS

INTRODUCTION

Congratulations! You've taken a big step toward achieving your best grade by purchasing *McGraw-Hill's 500 Psychology Questions*. We are here to help you improve your grades on classroom, midterm, and final exams. These 500 questions will help you study more effectively, use your preparation time wisely, and get the final grade you want.

This book gives you 500 multiple-choice questions that cover the most essential course material. Each question has a detailed answer explanation. These questions give you valuable independent practice to supplement your regular textbook and the groundwork you are already doing in the classroom.

You might be the kind of student who needs to study extra questions a few weeks before a big exam for a final review. Or you might be the kind of student who puts off preparing until right before a midterm or final. No matter what your preparation style, you will surely benefit from reviewing these 500 questions that closely parallel the content, format, and degree of difficulty of the questions found in typical college-level exams. These questions and their answer explanations are the ideal last-minute study tool for those final days before the test.

Remember the old saying "Practice makes perfect." If you practice with all the questions and answers in this book, we are certain that you will build the skills and confidence that are needed to ace your exams. Good luck!

—Editors of McGraw-Hill Education

McGraw-Hill's

500
Psychology
Questions

CHAPTER 1

Biological Basis of Behavior

Genetics

1. Gene expression is NOT impacted by which of the following factors?
   - (A) An organism's behaviors
   - (B) Nucleus size
   - (C) Timing of reproduction
   - (D) Temperature outside the cell
   - (E) Environment inside the cell

2. Which of the following defines the word *phenotype*?
   - (A) Gene transmission
   - (B) Gene that directs the development of a characteristic
   - (C) Pattern of genes in the chromosomes
   - (D) Traits, behaviors, and characteristics
   - (E) Part of a DNA molecule

3. How many chromosomes do cells in the human body typically contain?
   - (A) 92
   - (B) 46
   - (C) 23
   - (D) 12.5
   - (E) 6

4. What condition is needed for a recessive allele to be expressed as the organism's phenotype?
   - (A) A pairing with a dominant allele
   - (B) A pairing with an allele for a different gene that is also recessive
   - (C) A pairing with the same allele on the corresponding gene
   - (D) A pairing with any recessive allele in the DNA
   - (E) No pairing needed for the recessive allele to be expressed

5. Which concept describes the process of inheriting traits that is influenced by many different genes?
   (A) Natural selection
   (B) Gene transmission
   (C) Gene expression
   (D) Natural selection
   (E) Polygenetic inheritance

6. Which population of people is often studied to explore the impact of genetics?
   (A) Caucasian individuals
   (B) Individuals from developing countries
   (C) Younger siblings
   (D) Identical and fraternal twins
   (E) Childless adults

7. Which concept is used to explore the influence of genetics and environment with regard to a particular trait?
   (A) Susceptibility
   (B) Heritability
   (C) Natural selection
   (D) Monogenetic inheritance
   (E) Polygenetic inheritance

8. Which of the following factors have been found to influence psychological traits?
   (A) Genes
   (B) Family environment
   (C) Prenatal environment
   (D) Peer relationships
   (E) All of the above

9. Which of the following is identifiable through heritability estimates?
   (A) Amount of genetic similarity in a group
   (B) Influence of an individual's genes on his or her traits
   (C) Amount of environmental similarity in a group
   (D) The degree to which trait differences between individuals can be attributed to genes
   (E) The degree of heritability of a particular trait in a population

10. The concept that advantageous traits associated with survival and reproduction are more likely to be transmitted across generations is known as
    (A) polygenetic inheritance
    (B) natural selection
    (C) evolution
    (D) heredity
    (E) genetics

11. If an error occurs during reproduction resulting in a change in the structure or arrangement of the inherited DNA, this is called a(n)
    (A) selection
    (B) mutation
    (C) evolution
    (D) inheritance
    (E) genetic disorder

Neurobiology

12. Which types of cells carry information from the brain to muscles and glands in the body?
    (A) Atypical neurons
    (B) Sensory neurons
    (C) Interneurons
    (D) Motor neurons
    (E) Afferent neurons

13. Which part of a neuron carries information to other parts of the body and to other neurons?
    (A) Nucleus
    (B) Axon
    (C) Dendrite
    (D) Myelin sheath
    (E) Cell body

14. Which of these functions is NOT carried out by the glial cells?
    (A) Nourishment of neurons
    (B) Removal of waste from neurons
    (C) Control of nutrient supply
    (D) Creation of patterns of connections
    (E) Regulation of temperature of neurons

15. Serotonin, norepinephrine, and dopamine are examples of which type of chemical in the body?
    (A) Neurons
    (B) Neurotransmitters
    (C) Glutamate
    (D) Antagonists
    (E) Dendrites

16. Neurotransmitters send messages to other neurons by crossing what space?
    (A) Receptor site
    (B) Synaptic cleft
    (C) Cerebral cortex
    (D) Adrenal cortex
    (E) Hypothalamus

17. Which describes the main function of an SSRI, a class of medication commonly used to treat depression?
    (A) Enhance the release of serotonin
    (B) Slow the production of serotonin
    (C) Stop the production of serotonin
    (D) Block the reuptake of serotonin
    (E) Inhibit the production of serotonin

18. Which part of the nervous system is responsible for restoring the body back to normal functioning after arousal?
    (A) Central nervous system
    (B) Somatic nervous system
    (C) Sympathetic nervous system
    (D) Parasympathetic nervous system
    (E) Spinal cord

19. What function is the somatic nervous system responsible for?
    (A) Carrying motor messages and sensory information to and from the central nervous system
    (B) Receiving motor messages and sensory information from the autonomic nervous system
    (C) Processing information from the other parts of the nervous system
    (D) Mobilizing the body in times of activation
    (E) Restoring the body back to a resting state

20. A man is suddenly startled and then notices his heart rate has increased. Which nervous system was responsible for the increased heart rate?

(A) Central nervous system
(B) Somatic nervous system
(C) Sympathetic nervous system
(D) Parasympathetic nervous system
(E) Brain

21. The left brain is to _____ as the right brain is to _____.

(A) verbal; creative
(B) creative; verbal
(C) logic; objective
(D) objective; logic
(E) logic; verbal

22. Which system of the body is a system of glands that produce hormones?

(A) Nervous system
(B) Muscular system
(C) Endocrine system
(D) Reproductive system
(E) Lymphatic system

23. Which gland(s) is/are associated with metabolism and can cause irritability when too active and fatigue and depression when less active?

(A) Pineal gland
(B) Thyroid gland
(C) Pituitary gland
(D) Testes
(E) Adrenal gland

24. Which of the following is NOT an instrument used to study the brain?

(A) MRI (magnetic resonance imaging)
(B) PET scan (positron emission tomography)
(C) CT scan (computerized tomography)
(D) TMS (transcranial magnetic stimulation)
(E) fMRI (functional magnetic resonance imaging)

25. What is the adrenal gland mainly responsible for?
    (A) Releasing reproduction-related hormones
    (B) Releasing mood-related hormones
    (C) Releasing stress-related hormones
    (D) Releasing metabolism-related hormones
    (E) Releasing rest-related hormones

26. The chemicals produced in which part of the brain stem regulate sleep and wake cycles?
    (A) Medulla
    (B) Pons
    (C) Cerebellum
    (D) Thalamus
    (E) Midbrain

27. Which lobe of the cerebral hemisphere is involved in regulating emotion and behavior?
    (A) Frontal lobe
    (B) Temporal lobe
    (C) Occipital lobe
    (D) Parietal lobe
    (E) Cerebellum

28. If an individual has lost his or her sense of smell due to a traumatic brain injury, where did the injury likely occur?
    (A) Frontal lobe
    (B) Temporal lobe
    (C) Parietal lobe
    (D) Occipital lobe
    (E) Cerebellum

29. Which of the following is a function of the right hemisphere of the brain?
    (A) Speech development
    (B) Writing
    (C) Nonverbal tasks
    (D) Movement of the right side of the body
    (E) Information analysis

30. Which structure is part of the limbic system and is involved in evaluating emotional responses, including threats?

(A) Hippocampus
(B) Amygdala
(C) Hypothalamus
(D) Corpus callosum
(E) Spinal cord

31. The connections and patterns between neurons can change over time due to quality of relationships, individual experiences, an individual's age, and other internal and external experiences of the person. What is this concept called?

(A) Regeneration
(B) Neuroplasticity
(C) Lateralization
(D) Redevelopment
(E) Neural growth

32. Recognizing that it is cold outside and you should wear a coat involves which part of the brain?

(A) Prefrontal lobe
(B) Frontal lobe
(C) Temporal lobe
(D) Parietal lobe
(E) Occipital lobe

33. Which neurons carry sensory information to the brain?

(A) Motor neurons
(B) Interneurons
(C) Afferent neurons
(D) Associative neurons
(E) None of the above

34. When running a marathon, Maria felt great pain at mile 10, but at some point passed the pain threshold and ran without pain for the rest of the race. Which neurotransmitter was likely at high levels in her brain during this period?

(A) Serotonin
(B) Epinephrine
(C) Endorphins
(D) Dopamine
(E) Acetylcholine

35. Which lobe of the brain is involved in processing visual information?
    (A) Frontal lobe
    (B) Temporal lobe
    (C) Occipital lobe
    (D) Parietal lobe
    (E) Prefrontal lobe

36. Which hormone is associated with childbirth and also thought to be associated with falling in love?
    (A) Adrenaline
    (B) Oxytocin
    (C) Thyroxine
    (D) Estrogen
    (E) Insulin

37. Which gland is associated with the body's response to stress?
    (A) Thyroid gland
    (B) Pituitary gland
    (C) Reproductive gland
    (D) Adrenal gland
    (E) Pineal gland

38. The impulse of a neuron to fire is called
    (A) action potential
    (B) refractory period
    (C) resting potential
    (D) excitatory cells
    (E) inhibitory cells

39. Which type of chemical obstructs the action of neurotransmitters?
    (A) Serotonin
    (B) Agonist
    (C) Antagonist
    (D) GABA
    (E) None of the above

40. The somatic nervous system is to _____ as the autonomic nervous system is to _____.

    (A) involuntary; voluntary
    (B) voluntary; involuntary
    (C) sensation; perception
    (D) perception; sensation
    (E) involuntary; perception

41. Which part of the brain is the largest and includes the cerebellum and the limbic system?

    (A) Forebrain
    (B) Midbrain
    (C) Hindbrain
    (D) Frontal lobe
    (E) Occipital lobe

42. Which term refers to the different functions of the left side and the right side of the brain?

    (A) Bilateral stimulation
    (B) Lateralization
    (C) Mirroring
    (D) Neuroplasticity
    (E) None of the above

CHAPTER **2**

Sensation and Perception

Sensation

43. With regard to taste, what represents the smallest amount of a substance needed for it to be detected in one's food?

(A) Difference threshold
(B) Absolute threshold
(C) 1 gram of table salt per 600 quarts of water
(D) Noticeable threshold
(E) Sensory threshold

44. Caryn had her stereo on low and could barely hear it. She turned it up one notch but did not detect a change. She was able to hear the music clearly when she turned the stereo up two notches. In Caryn's case, two notches describe the smallest amount of input to recognize the change. What do the two notches represent in sensory terms?

(A) Difference threshold
(B) Absolute threshold
(C) Hearing threshold
(D) Sensory threshold
(E) Recognizable threshold

45. Tony used fractions to discover that humans have greater sensitivity to brightness than to weight. What rule did Tony use to make these comparisons?

(A) Fechner's law
(B) Weber's law
(C) Frequency theory
(D) Just noticeable difference
(E) Perceptual constancy

46. Pressure, temperature, and pain are what type of senses?

    (A) Auditory senses
    (B) Olfactory senses
    (C) Skin senses
    (D) Touch senses
    (E) Sight senses

47. A sense of smell is also known as

    (A) glomeruli
    (B) olfaction
    (C) odorants
    (D) anosmia
    (E) pheromones

48. Which name describes the taste that is savory; is associated with some meats, vegetables, and cheeses; and was the last taste receptor discovered?

    (A) Sweet
    (B) Salty
    (C) Bitter
    (D) Sour
    (E) Umami

49. The structures on the tongue that house the taste buds are called

    (A) receptor cells
    (B) papillae
    (C) molecules
    (D) tastants
    (E) saliva

50. When Keri blows a horn, she feels the vibration of the instrument. The vibration causes unseen air molecules to move and eventually enter the outer ear and progress toward the eardrum. What does Keri create by blowing the horn?

    (A) Sound waves
    (B) Speech
    (C) Tones
    (D) Frequency
    (E) Amplification of percussion

51. The frequency of a sound wave is measure in what unit?

(A) Octave

(B) Hertz

(C) Amplitude

(D) Decibel

(E) Timbre

52. Maria has twin sons. Maria can tell which son is calling her by the sound of each boy's voice. What concept allows Maria to differentiate their voices?

(A) Frequency

(B) Amplitude

(C) Timbre

(D) Pitch

(E) Octave

53. Which of the following describes the place theory related to pitch?

(A) Nerve impulses are related to frequencies of vibrations along the basilar membrane and determine pitch.

(B) Neurons determine pitch by noting the location on the basilar membrane where the messages are strongest.

(C) Neurons determine pitch by noting the size of the movement along the basilar membrane.

(D) Nerve impulses travel along the basilar membrane and determine pitch by the frequency of the impulses.

(E) Neurons determine pitch by noting the location on the cochlea where the messages are strongest and then sending the messages to the basilar membrane.

54. Hammer, anvil, and stirrup are parts related to which sense?

(A) Taste

(B) Sound

(C) Smell

(D) Touch

(E) Sight

55. A group of light wavelengths that the human eye can see goes from violet to red and includes the colors of the rainbow. What is this group called?

(A) The light spectrum
(B) The visual spectrum
(C) The visible spectrum
(D) The nanometer spectrum
(E) The trichromatic theory

56. Which structures in the retina respond to varying levels of light but NOT to color?

(A) Cones
(B) Rods
(C) Pupils
(D) Iris
(E) Fovea

57. How do messages from the retina reach the brain in order for one to actually see?

(A) Messages from rods and cones are sent to bipolar cells and are then sent to the axons, which carry the messages to the brain.
(B) Messages from bipolar cells activate the ganglion cells; then the axons of the ganglion cells come together to form an optical nerve that carries messages to the brain.
(C) The iris filters the amount of light and then passes messages to the rods and cones, which activate the ganglion cells that travel to the brain.
(D) Messages from the bipolar cells activate the axons to form an optical nerve that carries messages to the brain.
(E) Photoreceptors pass information to the ganglion, and the axons of the ganglion pass messages to the thalamus.

58. The axons of which cells come together to form the optic nerve?

(A) Rods
(B) Cones
(C) Bipolar cells
(D) Ganglion cells
(E) Fovea

59. Which structure of the eye is responsible for keen, sharp, and precise vision?

(A) Iris
(B) Cornea
(C) Retina
(D) Fovea
(E) Optic nerve

60. Which concept of color describes the vividness of hues?

(A) Saturation
(B) Brightness
(C) Achromatic
(D) Chromatic
(E) Trichromatic

61. Which concept of color allows one to differentiate black from gray?

(A) Saturation
(B) Hues
(C) Brightness
(D) Achromatic
(E) Chromatic

62. The trichromatic color vision principle states that there are three types of cones, each of which responds to different wavelengths of light, therefore allowing humans to see color. Which colors are associated with the trichromatic color vision theory?

(A) Red, green, yellow
(B) Red, blue, purple
(C) White, black, gray
(D) Red, blue, green
(E) Blue, green, yellow

63. According to which theory of color vision do color antagonists, including blue-yellow and red-green, operate in pairs to inform the perception of hue?

(A) Trichromatic color theory
(B) Opponent-process theory
(C) Huvich-Jameson theory
(D) Color-blindness theory
(E) Young-Helmholtz theory

64. Sandra stares at a green circle for 30 seconds and then shifts her vision to a plain white piece of paper. Initially, she sees a red circle on the page, although she knows the red circle is not there. What is the red circle?

    (A) An afterimage
    (B) A shadow
    (C) A light adaptation
    (D) A color adaptation
    (E) A blind spot

65. Evan is only able to see shades of light and dark that he describes as black, gray, and white. What condition does Evan have?

    (A) Trichromatic color-blindness
    (B) Dichromatic color-blindness
    (C) Monochromatic color-blindness
    (D) Protanopia color-blindness
    (E) Genetic color-blindness

Perception

66. Which statement describes the difference between sensation and perception?

    (A) Sensation is the sensory experience, while perception is how one creates the sensory experience.
    (B) Sensation is the making and interpretation of the perception process.
    (C) Sensation is the sensory experience, while perception is the meaning making and interpretation of the sensory experience.
    (D) Sensation is the stimulation of the senses, while perception is the period where the senses are not stimulated.
    (E) Sensation is the creation of sensory stimuli, while perception is the processing of that stimuli.

67. The idea that humans tend to perceive complete objects and overlook incomplete lines in figures is called

    (A) proximity
    (B) continuity
    (C) similarity
    (D) closure
    (E) contours

68. There are 10 straws that are grouped together in groups of 3 each, with 1 straw on its own. Which principle of perception states that people tend to perceive the 3 groups and 1 item rather than seeing the straws as 10 individual straws?

(A) Similarity
(B) Proximity
(C) Closure
(D) Continuity
(E) Contours

69. Tara has a photo showing her brother on a beach with the ocean in the background. Which concept of perception allows Tara to look at her brother apart from the ocean in the photo?

(A) Continuation
(B) Figure and ground
(C) Organization
(D) Distinction
(E) Constancy

70. What concept explains why we tend to perceive snow as white in daylight, nighttime, and the varying levels of sunlight in between?

(A) Object constancy
(B) Perceptual constancy
(C) Size constancy
(D) Perceptual organization
(E) Shape constancy

71. The concept that explains why parallel lines appear to converge as they get farther away from the viewer is called

(A) texture gradient
(B) aerial perspective
(C) linear perspective
(D) pictorial cues
(E) motion parallax

72. Which concept of perception explains why cubes that are drawn on a flat surface appear three-dimensional?

(A) Interposition
(B) Pictorial cues
(C) Superposition
(D) Aerial perspective
(E) Texture gradient

73. Which of the following is a real-life example of the concept of binocular disparity?
    (A) Drawing three-dimensional objects on flat surfaces
    (B) Looking through glasses with a blue lens and a red lens to make a movie appear three-dimensional
    (C) Viewing objects with only one eye and describing the object
    (D) Blocking the view of an object in the distance
    (E) Covering one eye to assess depth perception

74. George drew his own flip-book of a man lifting weights. Each page has a different drawing. When you flip through each page of the book quickly, it appears that the man is moving and lifting the weights. Which concept of perception does the flip-book illustrate?
    (A) Autokinetic illusion
    (B) Apparent movement
    (C) Motion parallax
    (D) Position constancy
    (E) Phi phenomenon

75. Which concept of perception allows one to see the object separate from its background?
    (A) Interposition
    (B) Figure and ground
    (C) Continuation
    (D) Distinction
    (E) Perceptual constancy

76. Misinterpretation of information in our surroundings may cause a(n)
    (A) sensation
    (B) perception
    (C) illusion
    (D) correspondence problem
    (E) visual search

77. Kayla writes her initials by making dots in the sand. Which concept of perception allows us to read Kayla's initials as whole letters even though they are a series of dots?
    (A) Proximity
    (B) Similarity
    (C) Continuity
    (D) Closure
    (E) None of the above

78. Which theory of psychology looks at the whole as greater than
the individual parts?

(A) Psychoanalytic theory
(B) Humanistic theory
(C) Behavioral theory
(D) Cognitive theory
(E) Gestalt theory

79. If you look at a drawing one way you see a face, and if you look at it
another way you see a lamp. What concept of perception allows for this
type of circumstance?

(A) Illusion
(B) Perceptual constancy
(C) Continuation
(D) Figure and ground
(E) Proximity

80. Tyler spots the church from blocks away. Even though data from his retina
show the church getting larger as he walks toward it, _____
allows for Tyler to perceive it as one size.

(A) figure and ground
(B) continuation
(C) perceptual constancy
(D) unconscious inference
(E) apparent movement

CHAPTER **3**

Consciousness

Sleep

81. Which stage of sleep is characterized by increased blood pressure and heart rate and other characteristics that mirror wakefulness?

(A) Stage 1
(B) Stage 2
(C) Stage 3
(D) Stage 4
(E) REM sleep

82. Emma fell asleep on the couch. Her roommate noticed her eyes rolling from side to side and her arm relax from its previous position. Then a dog barking outside quickly woke her. Which stage of sleep was Emma most likely in?

(A) Stage 1
(B) Stage 2
(C) Stage 3
(D) Stage 4
(E) REM sleep

83. Which statement most accurately describes the reason we dream?

(A) Humans dream for restorative processes.
(B) Humans dream to integrate latent and manifest content.
(C) We don't know the exact reason for dreaming, but there are many theories about why we dream and what dreams mean.
(D) Humans dream to rework events of their lives.
(E) Each person dreams for different reasons.

84. Karen has trouble falling asleep every night and tosses and turns for hours. Her sleep log shows she sleeps less than two hours per night. Which sleep disorder does Karen likely suffer from?

(A) Sleep terrors
(B) Sleep apnea
(C) Narcolepsy
(D) Insomnia
(E) Parasomnia

85. Which sleep disorder is genetically based and characterized by suddenly falling asleep in daytime hours and muscle weakness during moments of excitement?

(A) Sleep apnea
(B) Sleep walking disorder
(C) Insomnia
(D) Narcolepsy
(E) Parasomnia

86. As the age of an individual _____, the amount the person sleeps _____.

(A) increases; increases
(B) increases; decreases
(C) decreases; decreases
(D) decreases; increases
(E) none of the above

87. Which sleep disorder is characterized by difficulty breathing during sleep, resulting in frequent waking during the night?

(A) Narcolepsy
(B) Sleep apnea
(C) Insomnia
(D) Parasomnia
(E) Sleep terrors

88. Which stage of sleep is associated with slow delta waves?

(A) Stage 1
(B) Stage 2
(C) Stage 3
(D) Stage 4
(E) All of the above

89. How does the sleep cycle progress after stage 4?
   (A) Moving from stage 4 to REM sleep
   (B) Moving from stage 4 to stage 1
   (C) Moving from stage 4 back to stage 3
   (D) Remaining at stage 4
   (E) None of the above

90. According to Freud, what is the latent content of a dream?
   (A) Actual plot of the dream
   (B) Impact of the dream on consciousness
   (C) Underlying meaning of the dream
   (D) Repressed drives
   (E) A picture of the superego

91. Why is REM sleep also called paradoxical sleep?
   (A) REM sleep involves delta brain waves.
   (B) REM sleep involves delta, alpha, and beta waves.
   (C) REM sleep physiologically mirrors wakefulness.
   (D) REM sleep does not allow people to achieve rest.
   (E) REM sleep includes active dreaming.

92. Jet lag when traveling occurs because of a disruption of which innate cycle?
   (A) Sleep cycle
   (B) Light/dark cycle
   (C) Circadian rhythms
   (D) REM sleep
   (E) Ultradian rhythms

93. Which two outcomes are associated with sleep deprivation?
   (A) Increased accidents and compromised immune system
   (B) Workplace absenteeism and weight loss
   (C) Decreased need for sleep and compromised immune system
   (D) Weight loss and mood disorders
   (E) All of the above

94. Which answer choice is NOT associated with treating sleep difficulties?

 (A) Managing caffeine intake
 (B) Ensuring darkness in the bedroom
 (C) Limiting eating in the bedroom
 (D) Limiting watching television in the bedroom
 (E) Staying in bed all night even if sleep doesn't occur

95. During which stage of sleep is sleepwalking most likely to occur?

 (A) Stage 1
 (B) Stage 2
 (C) Stage 3
 (D) Stage 4
 (E) REM sleep

Other States of Consciousness

96. All of the following are altered states of consciousness EXCEPT

 (A) sleeping
 (B) meditation
 (C) alcohol intoxication
 (D) alertness
 (E) hypnosis

97. An individual's waking thoughts, feelings, and overall awareness of himself or herself and the surrounding environment is referred to as

 (A) alertness
 (B) consciousness
 (C) mindfulness
 (D) introspection
 (E) unconsciousness

98. Which state helps us to organize and perceive both the world around us and our own internal world without us knowing it?

 (A) Introspection
 (B) Dreaming
 (C) Cognitive unconscious
 (D) Consciousness
 (E) Alternate states of consciousness

99. Which of the following is a known effect of hypnosis?
- (A) Pain relief
- (B) Decreased depression
- (C) Increased physical strength
- (D) Elimination of free will
- (E) Improved memory

100. Which theory states that the hypnotic state separates us from our present experience and provides a feeling of being outside ourselves?
- (A) Suggestibility
- (B) Social influences
- (C) Dissociation
- (D) Chanting
- (E) Social cognitive

101. Brain activity during meditation mirrors brain activity during what other state of consciousness?
- (A) REM sleep
- (B) Relaxed wakefulness
- (C) Hypnosis
- (D) Stage 2 sleep
- (E) Depressant altered consciousness

102. Each morning Larry spends 30 minutes sitting quietly on the floor in focused attention on only his breath and a bell sound. Which of the following is NOT a typical result of this practice?
- (A) Decreased heart rate
- (B) Decreased respiratory rate
- (C) Decreased stress
- (D) Decreased need for sleep
- (E) Decreased susceptibility to illness

103. After drinking alcohol, one frequently experiences
- (A) decreased inhibition
- (B) increased social anxiety
- (C) decreased depressed mood
- (D) increased attention
- (E) decreased aggression

104. Which types of drugs are commonly used to treat attention-deficit/
hyperactivity disorder (ADHD) and are associated with increased energy
and decreased appetite?

(A) Depressants
(B) Stimulants
(C) Hallucinogens
(D) Barbiturates
(E) Sedatives

105. Which of the following is NOT associated with alcohol use?

(A) Legal age
(B) Genetics
(C) Family culture and norms
(D) Food preferences
(E) Decreased judgment

106. Tanya describes her boyfriend as having a "pill problem" and says
he uses prescription opiates daily. Which of the following describes
the most serious of the "pill problems" he could have?

(A) Opiate use
(B) Opiate abuse
(C) Opiate intoxication
(D) Opiate dependence
(E) Opiate tolerance

107. The phenomenon of needing more of the same substance to produce
the same effect is called

(A) drug intoxication
(B) drug tolerance
(C) drug intolerance
(D) drug abuse
(E) drug dependence

108. Which type of drug distorts visual and auditory perceptions and can
even lead to psychosis?

(A) Stimulant
(B) Depressant
(C) Hallucinogen
(D) Barbiturate
(E) Opiate

109. All of the following are effects of cocaine use EXCEPT
(A) blocking reabsorption of dopamine
(B) high energy and alertness
(C) intense cravings
(D) crashes, which include depressed mood
(E) calmness

110. After experimenting with drugs and alcohol in high school, Mary became dependent on opiates during college. Which of the following factors likely did NOT influence Mary's cycle into drug dependence?
(A) Genetic predisposition
(B) Environmental factors
(C) Recent traumas or difficult events
(D) Her prescription for fluoxetine (an SSRI)
(E) Peer network

CHAPTER 4

Learning and Memory

Learning

111. Which of these conditions is NOT a product of learning?

(A) Conditioned stimulus
(B) Conditioned response
(C) Unconditioned response
(D) Habituation
(E) Learned helplessness

112. In Pavlov's famous study on classical conditioning, which factor was the conditioned stimulus (CS)?

(A) Salivation
(B) Bell
(C) Meat powder
(D) The dogs
(E) Any food

113. Mr. Goodman attempts to keep squirrels away by placing chemicals on the trees that make the squirrels sick. The squirrels are noticeably avoiding his yard after two weeks. What are the US, CS, and CR in this scenario?

(A) The chemical; Mr. Goodman's trees; squirrels avoiding the trees
(B) Mr. Goodman's trees; the chemical; squirrels avoiding the trees
(C) Squirrels avoiding the trees; Mr. Goodman's trees; the chemical
(D) The chemical; squirrels avoiding the trees; Mr. Goodman's trees
(E) Mr. Goodman's trees; squirrels avoiding the trees; the chemical

114. Jason flies a great deal for work. Last year he had to fly while sick with the stomach flu. Now each time he gets on a plane he feels nauseous. What has a plane become for Jason?

(A) Conditioned stimulus
(B) Conditioned response
(C) Unconditioned stimulus
(D) Unconditioned response
(E) Extinction

115. In the case of Little Albert, an infant was presented with a rat. As the child reached for the rat, a researcher struck a steel bar making a loud, shocking noise. This was repeated numerous times. The child then showed fear when he saw the rat and fear of other similar animals. In this case, which factor is the unconditioned stimulus (US)?

(A) The rat
(B) The loud noise
(C) Fear
(D) Similar animals
(E) The child

116. Margo spent her summers at the town pool, where a group of kids continuously bullied her. She found herself crying in the bathroom and feeling sad. Now, as an adult, Margo is fearful of pools. She finds herself sweating, crying, dizzy, and quite uncomfortable at the sight or thought of a pool. She refuses to go to pools. It is possible, that through classical conditioning, Margo has developed which condition?

(A) Aversion
(B) Phobia
(C) Extinction
(D) Personality disorder
(E) Blocking effect

117. Which of the following describes spontaneous recovery?
   (A) After extinction, the conditioned stimulus is presented with the unconditioned stimulus and a small conditioned response occurs.
   (B) After extinction, the unconditioned stimulus continues to evoke the conditioned response.
   (C) After extinction, the conditioned stimulus is presented without the unconditioned stimulus and a small conditioned response occurs.
   (D) During extinction, the conditioned stimulus is presented without the unconditioned stimulus and no response occurs.
   (E) During extinction, the unconditioned stimulus is presented without the conditioned stimulus and a small conditioned response occurs.

118. A patient at a psychiatric clinic is being treated for his fear of bridges. He has made a hierarchy of his fears related to bridges and is learning to manage his fear and relax at the bottom of the hierarchy first. Which type of treatment is the patient likely participating in?
   (A) Psychopharmacology
   (B) Cognitive behavioral therapy
   (C) Systematic desensitization
   (D) Flooding
   (E) Meditation

119. Kerri will no longer eat shrimp. Many years ago she became quite ill after eating shrimp. When she sees or smells shrimp, Kerri gets immediately queasy. Which classical conditioning concept is happening for Kerri?
   (A) Food aversion
   (B) Taste aversion
   (C) Habituation
   (D) Second-order conditioning
   (E) Spontaneous recovery

120. Which of the following describes the conditions needed for extinction to occur?
   (A) The conditioned stimulus is presented repeatedly without the unconditioned stimulus.
   (B) The unconditioned stimulus is presented repeatedly without the conditioned stimulus.
   (C) The conditioned stimulus produces a changed conditioned response.
   (D) The unconditioned stimulus is paired with a different conditioned stimulus.
   (E) The conditioned stimulus produces the same conditioned response.

121. Which psychological disorder is thought to be associated with classical conditioning?

    (A) Depression
    (B) Phobias
    (C) Substance abuse
    (D) Bipolar disorder
    (E) Schizophrenia

122. When designing an experiment on classical conditioning, the _____ is to be paired with the _____, creating an unconditioned response (UR). This then allows the _____ to produce a conditioned response (CR).

    (A) CS; CR; CS
    (B) US; CR; CS
    (C) CR; CS; US
    (D) CS; US; CS
    (E) US; CS; US

123. Which type of learning occurs when behavior is followed by a stimulus that invites or discourages the behavior?

    (A) Classical conditioning
    (B) Operant conditioning
    (C) Latent learning
    (D) Higher-order conditioning
    (E) Reinforcer

124. When training their dog, the White family gives the dog a treat each time he sits when they ask him to. What does the dog treat represent?

    (A) Negative reinforcer
    (B) Positive reinforcer
    (C) Partial reinforcer
    (D) Positive punishment
    (E) Negative punishment

125. Each time Thomas talks back to his mother, he loses one hour of computer time. What does Thomas's consequence represent?

    (A) Negative reinforcer
    (B) Positive reinforcer
    (C) Partial reinforcer
    (D) Positive punishment
    (E) Negative punishment

126. Which of the following is NOT a condition needed for punishment to be effective?

(A) Occurring with consistency
(B) Occurring with proper strength
(C) Occurring shortly after behavior
(D) Steadily increasing in frequency
(E) Occurring each time the behavior occurs

127. In order to potty-train her daughter, Sharon began with rewarding her for just sitting on the toilet. Later, Sharon began rewarding her daughter for trying to use the toilet. Later, she rewarded her daughter each time she successfully used it. Which learning technique did Sharon use?

(A) Shaping
(B) Fixed-ratio reinforcement
(C) Interval reinforcement
(D) Latent learning
(E) Classical conditioning

128. Which concept of operant conditioning occurs when a behavior is followed by removing a negative stimulus in order to increase the frequency of the behavior?

(A) Negative reinforcement
(B) Positive reinforcement
(C) Negative punishment
(D) Positive punishment
(E) Variable-ratio reinforcement

129. Danna struggles with math and consistently scores C's and D's on her tests. At this point, she has stopped studying for her math tests because she believes that studying has no impact on her grades. What condition is Danna experiencing?

(A) Habituation
(B) Learned helplessness
(C) Vicarious conditioning
(D) Classical conditioning
(E) Operant conditioning

130. Phillip is a car salesman, and he receives a bonus after every 10 cars he sells. Which type of reinforcement schedule is this?

(A) Variable-ratio schedule
(B) Fixed-ratio schedule
(C) Partial reinforcement
(D) Negative reinforcement
(E) Interval schedule

131. Ryan has an older brother Ben. Each time Ben gets in trouble at school, he is not allowed to go out with his friends for an entire week. Ryan does not want this consequence, so he makes sure not to get in trouble at school. Which type of learning has Ryan likely experienced?

(A) Vicarious learning
(B) Shaping
(C) Latent learning
(D) Cognitive learning
(E) Prepared learning

132. Jamal moved to a new city for a summer internship. After living there for one month, he has developed a mental representation of his new neighborhood. What has Jamal developed?

(A) Mirror neurons
(B) Vicarious learning
(C) Cognitive map
(D) Insight
(E) Social learning

133. Which statement is true about learning in organisms?

(A) Nonhuman organisms are not capable of operant conditioning.
(B) Nonhuman organisms are not capable of classical conditioning.
(C) Humans are the only organisms capable of latent learning.
(D) Humans and nonhumans are capable of operant conditioning, classical conditioning, and latent learning.
(E) Humans and nonhumans are not capable of operant conditioning, classical conditioning, or latent learning.

134. After being bitten by a dog, Sabrina developed an intense fear of dogs. Now, four years later, she is able to be around dogs and pet dogs without any distress. What process has taken place that eliminated Sabrina's fear?

(A) Spontaneous recovery
(B) Extinction
(C) Aversion
(D) Blocking effect
(E) Systematic desensitization

135. If Sarah wants to teach her dog to fetch a ball, which form of learning will she likely use?

(A) Classical conditioning
(B) Operant conditioning
(C) Latent learning
(D) Vicarious learning
(E) Cognitive learning

136. Which type of learning occurs without reinforcement?

(A) Operant conditioning
(B) Latent learning
(C) Negative reinforcer
(D) Shaping
(E) Extinction

Memory

137. Carrie returned from vacation and told her family a detailed description of the highlights. Carrie did not keep a journal but remembered the highlights easily. What is this process called?

(A) Recall
(B) Acquisition
(C) Intentional learning
(D) Incidental learning
(E) Short-term memory

138. The three steps of the memory process are

(A) recall, encoding, retrieval
(B) encoding, acquisition, storage
(C) encoding, storage, retrieval
(D) acquisition, storage, recall
(E) encoding, storage, acquisition

139. Troy is faced with memorizing a list of words that are in alphabetical order. There is a word that begins with each letter of the alphabet. After hearing the list, which words is Troy most likely to remember?

(A) Words that begin with letters at the beginning and end of the alphabet

(B) Words that begin with letters at the beginning of the alphabet

(C) Words that begin with letters at the end of the alphabet

(D) Words that begin with letters in the middle of the alphabet

(E) 10 words from the list with no pattern

140. Primacy effect is to _____ as recency effect is to _____.

(A) short-term memory; long-term memory

(B) long-term memory; short-term memory

(C) short-term memory; short-term memory

(D) long-term memory; long-term memory

(E) short-term memory; free recall

141. Brittney needs to memorize the following code to access a secure computer:

1244001782346557

What strategy will help Brittney increase her chances of remembering the code?

(A) Recall

(B) Maintenance rehearsal

(C) Chunking

(D) Deep processing

(E) Mnemonics

142. Students in piano class are taught to remember the following sentence:

Every Good Boy Deserves Fudge

The first letter of each word in the sentence describes the order of musical notes. Which memory strategy is used in this example?

(A) Chunking

(B) Maintenance rehearsal

(C) Shallow processing

(D) Mnemonics

(E) Deep processing

143. Which of the following memory strategies is NOT effective for creating long-term memories?

(A) Mnemonics
(B) Deep processing
(C) Maintenance rehearsal without learning
(D) Chunking
(E) Recall

144. Which two factors are critical in the process of storing information in long-term memory?

(A) Recall and understanding
(B) Learning and understanding
(C) Attention and learning
(D) Attention and processing
(E) Learning and retrieval

145. Because it refers to memories or thoughts that are currently activated and being used, short-term memory is also called

(A) present memory
(B) working memory
(C) attention
(D) schemata
(E) procedural memory

146. When Laurie returned to her college campus 10 years after graduation, she found herself flooded with memories that she did not even know she had. What did the campus visit represent to Laurie?

(A) Implicit memories
(B) Retrieval cues
(C) Memory traces
(D) Schema
(E) Semantic memories

147. Adrian was given a list of groceries to buy, but when he got to the store he remembered only the first three items on the list and the last item on the list. Which memory concept describes Adrian's experience?

(A) Primacy effect
(B) Recency effect
(C) Free recall
(D) Working memory
(E) Primacy effect and recency effect

148. Which part of the brain is responsible for storing emotional memories?

    (A) Frontal lobe
    (B) Prefrontal cortex
    (C) Amygdala
    (D) Hippocampus
    (E) Motor cortex

149. After his bike accident, Sean was diagnosed with retrograde amnesia. What is Sean's experience of memory?

    (A) He has no ability to create new memories.
    (B) He has no ability to remember the three years of his life leading up to the accident.
    (C) He has no ability to remember anything about his life.
    (D) He has short-term memory but no long-term memory.
    (E) He has long-term memory but no short-term memory.

150. The addition of new information can interfere with already stored information, leading to forgetting. What is this phenomena called?

    (A) Decay theory
    (B) Retroactive interference
    (C) Proactive interference
    (D) Amnesia
    (E) Forgetting curve

151. Tyler memorized a monologue to present during a high school performance. When he tried to share the monologue with his friends from law school he could no longer remember it. What has likely happened to his memories of the monologue?

    (A) Decay theory
    (B) A very small retention interval
    (C) Intrusion errors
    (D) Amnesia
    (E) Proactive interference

152. Short-term memory is to _____ as long-term memory is to _____.

    (A) attention; understanding
    (B) understanding; attention
    (C) meaning; understanding
    (D) attention; rehearsal
    (E) learning; understanding

153. The ability to ride a bike after being taught is an example of a(n)
   (A) emotional memory
   (B) episodic memory
   (C) semantic memory
   (D) procedural memory
   (E) working memory

154. Valari listened to Mozart while studying for the test. Which is the best condition for Valari to take the test?
   (A) Take the test in complete silence
   (B) Take the test in the library
   (C) Take the test while listening to Mozart
   (D) Take the test while listening to any classical music
   (E) Take the test while watching television

155. Which of the following describes the concept of context reinstatement?
   (A) Increasing memory retrieval by re-creating the environment where the memory occurred
   (B) Increasing memory retrieval by re-creating the state of mind present when the memory occurred
   (C) Increasing memory retrieval by decreasing retroactive interference
   (D) Increasing memory retrieval by increasing amount of rote rehearsal
   (E) Increasing memory retrieval by decreasing proactive interference

156. Which of the following is NOT a strategy to reduce forgetting?
   (A) Using retrieval cues
   (B) Making connections between information and other things you know
   (C) Remaining focused
   (D) Using imagery
   (E) Using hypnosis

157. Which memories are hidden from consciousness and may sometimes be created when an individual experiences a trauma?
   (A) Flashbulb memories
   (B) Episodic memories
   (C) Semantic memories
   (D) Procedural memories
   (E) Repressed memories

158. When Emma recalls the hurricane she experienced as a child, she has vivid images of what happened and immediately becomes anxious. What type of memory is Emma likely experiencing?

(A) Procedural memory
(B) Episodic memory
(C) Flashbulb memory
(D) Semantic memory
(E) Repressed memory

159. Which type of memory is NOT consciously recalled but is revealed through an individual's behaviors or responses?

(A) Semantic memory
(B) Flashbulb memory
(C) Episodic memory
(D) Explicit memory
(E) Implicit memory

160. Which memory strategy includes linking new memories to old memories that are already stored in long-term memory?

(A) Rote rehearsal
(B) Maintenance rehearsal
(C) Elaborate rehearsal
(D) Mnemonics
(E) None of the above

161. Long-term memory includes all of these types of memories EXCEPT

(A) semantic memory
(B) implicit memory
(C) autobiographical memory
(D) explicit memory
(E) working memory

162. Which strategy is Keisha using when she repeats a phone number three times before dialing?

(A) Elaborate rehearsal
(B) Chunking
(C) Mnemonics
(D) Maintenance rehearsal
(E) Explicit memory

163. A combination of all types of long-term memories contributes to one's
_____ about the world but may also distort memories.

(A) interactions
(B) schema
(C) relationships
(D) short-term memories
(E) none of the above

164. Barry witnessed a robbery and participated in a police interview to identify
the perpetrator. The next day, Barry viewed a news report on the robbery
and his memory about the appearance of the perpetrator changed.
Which memory error does this describe?

(A) Amnesia
(B) Retrograde amnesia
(C) Proactive interference
(D) Retroactive interference
(E) Decay

165. During long, drawn-out court cases, witnesses' stories sometimes change
over their numerous interviews and testifying. Which phenomenon
of forgetting may explain this experience?

(A) Amnesia
(B) Retrograde amnesia
(C) Decay
(D) Proactive interference
(E) Reconstruction

166. A male college student studies theories of the philosophy of the mind
by reading and rereading the information. The student is aware that his
understanding of the concepts is limited. Which cause of forgetting may
limit the student's recall on the exam?

(A) Decay
(B) Interference
(C) Encoding
(D) Retrieval
(E) Brain injury

167. Phillip has very vivid memories, some of which are sensory, of the moment he learned of his father's death. These memories are sometimes triggered. What type of memory is Phillip experiencing?

(A) Flashbulb memory
(B) Working memory
(C) Semantic memory
(D) Autobiographical memory
(E) Episodic memory

CHAPTER **5**

Cognition and Language

Cognition

168. Language, concepts, and images are all foundations of

(A) thought
(B) memory
(C) speech
(D) perception
(E) communication

169. When asked to picture her childhood home, Nita conjures up a visualization of what home looks like. What is this visualization called?

(A) Symbolic representation
(B) Analogical representation
(C) Schema
(D) Prototype
(E) Concept

170. What is a mental representation that is based on association or relationship with other known things but does not share specific qualities of what it represents?

(A) Cognitive schema
(B) Prototype
(C) Mental image
(D) Analogical representation
(E) Symbolic representation

171. When Ryan asked his 20 classmates the first thing that came to mind when he said "house pet," 15 of his classmates said "dog." What kind of mental model is "dog" in this case?
    (A) An image
    (B) A prototype
    (C) A concept
    (D) A mental representation
    (E) An experience

172. In the process of cognition, humans mentally categorize objects, people, and life events. What is this categorization called?
    (A) Mental representations
    (B) Mental images
    (C) Concepts
    (D) Prototypes
    (E) Sensory clues

173. Julian's physician gave him the treatment outcome data of two courses of treatment to choose from to combat acne. One set of outcome data describes success rates, while the other describes failure rates. What is likely to inform Julian's decision-making process?
    (A) Mental images
    (B) Mental representations
    (C) Framing
    (D) Prototypes
    (E) Compensatory model

174. What is the disadvantage to using heuristics when problem solving?
    (A) Mistakes may be made due to the simplification of the problem.
    (B) Making the decision may be a long, drawn-out problem.
    (C) Mistakes may be made due to the overanalysis of the problem.
    (D) Using heuristics may be influenced by personal background.
    (E) Mistakes may be made by building subgoals.

175. Which of the following is NOT a problem-solving strategy?
    (A) Trial and error
    (B) Information retrieval
    (C) Algorithms
    (D) Fixedness
    (E) Working backward

176. Which of the following is NOT a barrier to problem solving?

(A) Mental sets

(B) Functional fixedness

(C) Assumptions

(D) Expertise

(E) Motivation

177. To determine if she should increase her exercise to increase her energy, Jen counted in her head how many days in the last month she had high energy and if those days were associated with exercise. Which judgment-related strategy did Jen use?

(A) Representative heuristics

(B) Availability heuristics

(C) Confirmation bias

(D) Framing

(E) Frequency

178. Which problem-solving strategy could someone use to calculate the number of possible outcomes of rolling five die?

(A) Trial and error

(B) Working backward

(C) Subgoal

(D) Algorithm

(E) Information retrieval

179. After having a snow-related car accident, Carlos decided the accident was inevitable because of his decision to drive in the snow. Which type of decision-making thinking is Carlos experiencing?

(A) Confirmation bias

(B) Overconfidence effect

(C) Minimizing risk

(D) Risky thinking

(E) Hindsight bias

180. In cognition a(n) _____ is an example of a concept.

(A) idea

(B) schema

(C) mental representation

(D) prototype

(E) none of the above

181. Charles is traveling to Los Angeles. Although he's never been there, he has beliefs, assumptions, and expectations about what it is like in Los Angeles that he got from friends, books, movies, and other information sources. What are these beliefs and ideas that Charles has?

    (A) Prototypes
    (B) Mental representations
    (C) Cognitive schemas
    (D) Mental images
    (E) Analogical representations

182. Which error in reasoning is a result of attaching more weight to evidence that is consistent with one's beliefs?

    (A) Hindsight bias
    (B) Confirmation bias
    (C) Judgment bias
    (D) Deduction bias
    (E) None of the above

183. When Sharon makes a decision based on what's most easily accessible in her memory, which decision-making strategy is she using?

    (A) Confirmation bias
    (B) The availability heuristic
    (C) Compensatory model
    (D) Working backward
    (E) None of the above

Language

184. Which structure of language is on top of the language hierarchy?

    (A) Phoneme
    (B) Morpheme
    (C) Word
    (D) Phrase
    (E) Sentence

185. What are the basic sounds that make up language?

    (A) Phonemes
    (B) Morphemes
    (C) Words
    (D) Phrases
    (E) Sentences

186. What is the set of principles of grouping words into phrases and sentences?

(A) Noun phrase
(B) Verb phrase
(C) Syntax
(D) Linguistic determinism
(E) Semantics

187. At what age does a human being develop openness to hearing and digesting language and cues of language?

(A) 2 years
(B) 18 months
(C) 1 year
(D) 6 months
(E) Birth

188. When a verb describes the action in a sentence, this is the verb's

(A) determinism
(B) meaning
(C) semantic role
(D) syntax
(E) grammar

189. When Thomas says the accident scene is "burned into his memory," it evokes a certain thought for those who understand the metaphor. What does this use of language demonstrate?

(A) The interplay between thought and language
(B) The influence of culture on language
(C) The influence of metaphor on feelings
(D) The interplay between feelings and thoughts
(E) The influence of language on the use of metaphors

190. The rare cases where a child is not exposed to language early in life due to neglect or other circumstances and subsequently has much difficulty developing language skills demonstrate the importance of _____ in language development.

(A) intelligence
(B) biology
(C) cognition
(D) environment
(E) learning

191. The underlying meaning of a sentence is considered its

    (A) surface structure
    (B) deep structure
    (C) phrase structure
    (D) grammatical structure
    (E) sentence structure

192. The fact that the human language has meaning indicates that it is

    (A) heuristic
    (B) semantic
    (C) cognitive
    (D) variable
    (E) communicative

193. Kendra is studying Spanish and has trouble rolling her *r* because it is not a sound of the English language. Which language unit is Kendra struggling with?

    (A) Sentence
    (B) Phrase
    (C) Word
    (D) Morpheme
    (E) Phoneme

194. In the structure of language, the prefix *un-* is called a

    (A) sentence
    (B) phrase
    (C) word
    (D) morpheme
    (E) phoneme

195. One hypothesis around language states that the language that one speaks profoundly influences

    (A) feeling states
    (B) cognitive functioning
    (C) the ability to learn another language
    (D) patterns of thinking
    (E) problem-solving skills

196. Across cultures, children tend to acquire complex language skills before which age?

(A) One year old
(B) Two years old
(C) Three years old
(D) Four years old
(E) Five years old

197. Whorf's theory of linguistic relativity describes

(A) the ways language influences thinking
(B) the development of language from infancy
(C) the development of bilingualism
(D) the ways language influences intelligence
(E) cultural influences on language

198. Which concept is demonstrated by the expression "she slept like a log"?

(A) The linear relationship of thinking and language
(B) The rigid relationship between thinking and language
(C) The pattern of thinking and language
(D) The interplay and adaptable relationship of thinking and language
(E) None of the above

CHAPTER 6

Intelligence

Intelligence

199. Which of the following is NOT one of the multiple intelligences in Howard Gardner's theory?

(A) Musical
(B) Linguistic
(C) Spatial
(D) Historical
(E) Logical-mathematical

200. Phillip has been diagnosed with pervasive developmental disorder and has impaired social functioning but can recite sports statistics for the past two decades. This ability is likely due to

(A) cognitive capacities
(B) high IQ
(C) savant syndrome
(D) mental retardation
(E) emotional intelligence

201. All of the following are aspects of emotional intelligence EXCEPT

(A) perceiving emotions of others
(B) using emotions
(C) understanding emotions
(D) describing emotions
(E) managing emotions

202. Tacit knowledge contributes to which type of intelligence?

(A) Emotional intelligence
(B) Analytical intelligence
(C) Practical intelligence
(D) Creative intelligence
(E) Fluid intelligence

203. Verbal skills, cognitive skills, and reasoning make up which type of intelligence?

(A) Practical intelligence
(B) Analytical intelligence
(C) Crystallized intelligence
(D) Fluid intelligence
(E) Emotional intelligence

204. Included in _____ is the ability to solve emerging problems or issues and use spatial and visual imagery.

(A) emotional intelligence
(B) fluid intelligence
(C) crystallized intelligence
(D) analytical intelligence
(E) emotional intelligence

205. Initial intelligence tests calculated the ratio of a child's _____ to his or her _____.

(A) mental age; chronological age
(B) chronological age; mental age
(C) mental age; test score
(D) chronological age; test score
(E) mental age; intelligence quotient

206. Which type of mental ability is NOT measured on a Stanford-Binet IQ test?

(A) Verbal reasoning
(B) Abstract and visual reasoning
(C) Quantitative reasoning
(D) Long-term memory
(E) Short-term memory

207. Which type of intelligence is typically measured by intelligence tests?

(A) Analytical intelligence
(B) Practical intelligence
(C) Multiple intelligences
(D) Emotional intelligence
(E) Creative intelligence

208. Pauline noticed that her boss was quite upset. She could see and understand why he was upset and chose to keep her distance for a few days. Although this made Pauline feel tense, she did not show it to her own employees and presented herself professionally during this time. One may say that Pauline shows the abilities of

(A) multiple intelligences
(B) emotional intelligence
(C) tacit knowledge
(D) analytical intelligence
(E) practical intelligence

209. When Henry is tired after work, he finds it difficult to think quickly and to solve some of the new issues that emerge when raising toddlers. Which type of intelligence is being impacted by Henry's fatigue?

(A) Emotional intelligence
(B) Crystallized intelligence
(C) Fluid intelligence
(D) Analytical intelligence
(E) Practical intelligence

210. Which two abilities do the Wechsler Adult Intelligence tests measure?

(A) Cognitive and spatial abilities
(B) Intellectual and verbal abilities
(C) Verbal and performance abilities
(D) Verbal and mental abilities
(E) Spatial and performance abilities

211. The fact that a boy's intelligence test at age 5 yields very similar results at age 10 indicates that test's

(A) content validity
(B) criterion-related validity
(C) predictive validity
(D) split-half reliability
(E) test-retest reliability

212. Which is NOT a limitation of intelligence tests?
- (A) Possible cultural bias
- (B) Self-fulfilling prophecy
- (C) Labeling
- (D) Genetic influence of intelligence
- (E) Small skill set measurement

213. Which factors that influence intelligence include access to resources, nutrition, and intellectual stimulation?
- (A) Genetic factors
- (B) Environmental factors
- (C) Hereditary factors
- (D) Cultural factors
- (E) Test-taking factors

214. An individual with mental retardation shows deficiencies in which two arenas?
- (A) Intelligence and problem-solving abilities
- (B) Adaptive functioning and self-care
- (C) Test-taking abilities and self-care
- (D) Intelligence and adaptive functioning
- (E) Adaptive functioning and practical intelligence

215. An individual with a very high IQ who also shows leadership and creativity may be considered
- (A) an intelligent person
- (B) a gifted person
- (C) a savant
- (D) a genius
- (E) a prodigy

216. Which pair shows the highest correlation of IQ scores?
- (A) Siblings raised together
- (B) Fraternal twins raised apart
- (C) Fraternal twins raised together
- (D) Identical twins raised apart
- (E) Child raised with same-sex parent

217. What factor likely influences the data in which men score higher on visual spatial aspects of intelligence tests?

(A) Socioeconomic status
(B) Cultural environment
(C) Teacher qualities
(D) Stereotypes
(E) Nutrition

218. Which statement about IQ tests indicates their predictive validity?

(A) High scores on IQ tests correlate with workplace and school difficulties.
(B) High scores on IQ tests correlate with workplace and school success.
(C) High scores on IQ tests in childhood predict high scores on IQ tests in adulthood.
(D) High scores on IQ tests correlate with high scores on all tests.
(E) High scores on one-half of an IQ test indicate high scores on the other half.

219. Which types of intelligence make up the triarchic theory of intelligence?

(A) Analytical, creative, and practical intelligences
(B) Analytical, practical, and emotional intelligences
(C) Creative, emotional, and practical intelligences
(D) Crystallized, fluid, and analytical intelligences
(E) Crystallized, fluid, and creative intelligences

220. Toby has strong relationship skills and is aware of his feelings and how to manage them. He uses his feelings to help himself and is aware of the feelings of others. Which type of intelligence does Toby display?

(A) Analytical intelligence
(B) Emotional intelligence
(C) Practical intelligence
(D) Creative intelligence
(E) Fluid intelligence

221. Verbal abilities and perceptual skills are measured on which type of intelligence test?

(A) Stanford-Binet IQ test
(B) Binet test
(C) Wechsler Adult Intelligence Scale–Third Edition test
(D) Performance test
(E) None of the above

222. Which type of intelligence test does NOT rely on language skills?

    (A) Stanford-Binet IQ test

    (B) Group test

    (C) Wechsler Adult Intelligence Scale–Third Edition test

    (D) Performance test

    (E) Culture-fair test

223. An individual who can remember every word he or she has ever read but has below-average scores on IQ tests displays which quality?

    (A) Giftedness

    (B) Emotional intelligence

    (C) Savant syndrome

    (D) Pervasive developmental disorder

    (E) Linguistic intelligence

CHAPTER 7

Motivation and Emotion

Motivation

224. A(n) _____ is a need or desire that incites goal-directed behavior by an organism.

(A) feeling
(B) drive
(C) motive
(D) behavior
(E) emotion

225. Which term refers to the equilibrium, or balance, an individual achieves by various types of self-regulation?

(A) Motive
(B) Drive
(C) Homeostasis
(D) Instinct
(E) Thermoregulation

226. According to the drive-reduction theory, the drive to eat can come from

(A) an internal instinct
(B) a state of tension caused by a change in homeostasis
(C) a state of tension caused by innate drives
(D) an attempt to reduce hunger
(E) an attempt to achieve homeostasis

227. According to the arousal theory, what is the root of motivation?

    (A) To reduce arousal
    (B) To increase arousal
    (C) To reach optimum arousal
    (D) To track changes in arousal
    (E) To keep arousal at a steady baseline level

228. External stimuli that provoke behavior are called

    (A) drives
    (B) instincts
    (C) incentives
    (D) motives
    (E) feelings

229. A salesman's motivation to work more and sell more to make a bonus is an example of

    (A) drive
    (B) intrinsic motivation
    (C) extrinsic motivation
    (D) unconscious motivation
    (E) goal-directed motivation

230. Which of the following is LEAST LIKELY to trigger the thirst drive?

    (A) Level of internal body fluids
    (B) Belief about the importance of fluids
    (C) Availability of a water fountain
    (D) Time of day
    (E) A commercial for spring water

231. Which is the only human motivation that is inherently social?

    (A) Hunger
    (B) Thirst
    (C) Sleep
    (D) Sex
    (E) Temperature regulation

232. Which part of the body is NOT involved in regulating hunger and food intake?

(A) Hypothalamus
(B) Spinal cord
(C) Liver
(D) Stomach walls
(E) Pituitary gland

233. Arousal theory is to _____ as drive-reduction theory is to _____.

(A) optimal arousal level; return to homeostasis
(B) return to homeostasis; optimal arousal level
(C) minimizing arousal; minimizing homeostasis
(D) facilitating arousal; facilitating homeostasis
(E) optimal arousal level; reduction of time in homeostasis

234. In order to maximize performance, complicated tasks require _____ and simple tasks require _____.

(A) high arousal; low arousal
(B) low arousal; high arousal
(C) moderate arousal; high arousal
(D) high arousal; high arousal
(E) low arousal; low arousal

235. Shane had no initial interest in trying a new neighborhood restaurant, but he saw an advertisement for the restaurant so frequently that he became interested. For Shane, the restaurant ad was a(n)

(A) motive
(B) drive
(C) feeling
(D) instinct
(E) incentive

236. Each morning four-year-old Chloe gets up and plays make-believe with her stuffed animals and the other toys in her bedroom. What type of motivation is this behavior called?

(A) Extrinsic motivation
(B) Intrinsic motivation
(C) Unconscious motivation
(D) Drive-reduction motivation
(E) Arousal-based motivation

237. Which of the following factors does NOT influence the motivation to eat, overeat, or restrict eating?

(A) Cultural factors
(B) Biological factors
(C) Environmental factors
(D) Secondary drive factors
(E) Psychological factors

238. Which of the following is NOT a cultural influence on eating behaviors?

(A) The amount we eat
(B) The times we eat
(C) The body image ideal
(D) Our memory of our last meal
(E) The ritual around eating

239. Which is a key difference in human sexual behavior versus sexual behavior in other organisms?

(A) Human sexual behavior is primarily biologically driven.
(B) Human sexual behavior is heavily influenced by learning.
(C) Human sexual behavior is driven by hormones.
(D) Timing is critical in human sexual behavior.
(E) Human sexual behavior is primarily automatic.

240. What is the correct order of the human sexual response cycle?

(A) Resolution, excitement, plateau, orgasm
(B) Excitement, plateau, orgasm, resolution
(C) Plateau, excitement, orgasm, resolution
(D) Excitement, orgasm, plateau, resolution
(E) Plateau, orgasm, resolution, excitement

241. All of the following is true about aggression in humans EXCEPT

(A) aggression is externally triggered
(B) aggression is learned
(C) aggression is influenced by gender
(D) aggression is influenced by intent
(E) culture is not a factor in aggression

242. All of the following are types of human motivation EXCEPT

(A) achievement
(B) belonging
(C) emotion
(D) exploration
(E) safety

243. What is at the top of Maslow's hierarchy of needs?

(A) Self-actualization needs
(B) Esteem needs
(C) Belongingness needs
(D) Safety needs
(E) Physiological needs

244. Natalie recently lost her job, and her home may be foreclosed. She has resources for food and water. In the meantime, Natalie would like to find a significant other. Using Maslow's hierarchy, which level does Natalie likely need to address before moving toward finding a significant other?

(A) Physiological needs
(B) Safety needs
(C) Belongingness needs
(D) Esteem needs
(E) Self-actualization needs

Emotion

245. All of the following contribute to the meaning of emotions EXCEPT

(A) affective responses
(B) the way we feel
(C) physiology
(D) intelligence
(E) behavior

246. Which of the following is NOT one of Plutchik's basic emotions?

(A) Fear
(B) Sadness
(C) Pain
(D) Surprise
(E) Anger

247. Researchers found that the expression of emotion varied across cultures when individuals were shown certain images. This phenomenon is likely due to

(A) varying perception of emotions
(B) display rules
(C) biological predisposition
(D) mood states
(E) affective responses

248. The James-Lange theory of emotion states that the experience of emotion is dictated by the

(A) experience of the physiological changes created by the stimuli
(B) cognitive experience of the stimuli
(C) physiological and neurobiological changes created by the stimuli simultaneously
(D) environmental clues created by the stimuli
(E) neurobiological changes created by the stimuli

249. According to the Cannon-Bard theory, which two factors are simultaneously activated by environmental stimuli?

(A) Cognitive and emotional responses
(B) Emotions and physiological responses
(C) Physiological and cognitive responses
(D) Physiological and environmental responses
(E) Cognitive and neurobiological responses

CHAPTER 8

Social Psychology

Social Cognition

250. Social psychology is the study of how an individual's thoughts, feelings, and behaviors are influenced by

(A) beliefs about self
(B) attributions about self
(C) actions and qualities of others
(D) behaviors of family members
(E) attitudes of others

251. The young man Carla is interviewing appears quite nervous, and Carla has a few theories about why. What are these theories called?

(A) Attitudes
(B) Behaviors
(C) Cognitions
(D) Attributions
(E) Schemas

252. Although Paul has been kind and funny when they have interacted after their first meeting, Shawn has difficulty believing he is kind and funny because during their first meeting Paul was short and uninterested. What phenomenon does this situation describe?

(A) Stereotyping
(B) Primacy effect
(C) Distinctiveness
(D) Attribution
(E) Cognitive dissonance

253. Schemata help humans form impressions by
  (A) evaluating relevant data
  (B) allowing for organization of information into categories and influencing the interpreting and remembering of information
  (C) prioritizing early information over later information
  (D) using a set of categories that is believed to be shared by members of a certain group
  (E) answering questions about the causes of behaviors

254. Incorrect attribution of a behavior to personal qualities with lack of attention to situational qualities is called
  (A) judgment error
  (B) fundamental attribution error
  (C) perception bias
  (D) just-world hypothesis
  (E) stereotyping

255. A person's relatively stable thoughts, feelings, and behaviors about an individual, group, or issue makes up his or her
  (A) belief
  (B) attitude
  (C) attribution
  (D) cognition
  (E) self-fulfilling prophecy

256. A teacher's belief that male students will do better on math tests may influence the males in the class to, in fact, produce higher test scores. Which phenomenon does this situation describe?
  (A) Just-world hypothesis
  (B) Defensive attribution
  (C) Prejudice
  (D) Stereotype
  (E) Self-fulfilling prophecy

257. Julie was particularly upset when she lost her dog because she believed she was a good person and because she was a good person bad things should not happen to her. Which attribution error did Julie exhibit?
  (A) Fundamental attribution error
  (B) Just-world hypothesis
  (C) Distinctiveness
  (D) Defensive attribution error
  (E) Cognitive dissonance

258. A person who has had negative experiences with individuals from a different cultural background than his or her own may categorize this group of individuals in a certain way. What is this person doing?

(A) Stereotyping
(B) Using attribution
(C) Using the self-fulfilling prophecy
(D) Forming a cognition
(E) Forming an attitude

259. Mr. Palmer believes strongly that his son Corey acts differently when around his friends in order to show off. What is Mr. Palmer's belief about Corey's behavior?

(A) An attribution
(B) An attitude
(C) A cognition
(D) A prejudice
(E) A schema

260. What type of attribution error occurs when an individual attributes his or her successes to individual qualities and efforts while attributing failures to systemic or external circumstances?

(A) Just-world hypothesis
(B) Defensive attribution error
(C) Fundamental attribution error
(D) Cultural attribution error
(E) Error in consensus

261. Which of the following is NOT known to be a factor in attraction?

(A) Physical attractiveness
(B) Similarity
(C) Proximity
(D) Trust
(E) Equitable exchange

262. When exploring attributions of people's behaviors, it is critical to pay attention to

(A) stereotypes
(B) culture
(C) attitudes
(D) schemata
(E) cognitions

263. Which example describes a fundamental attribution error?

(A) Deciding that half of the subjects must be very smart due to test results without the knowledge that those subjects were given intense preparation for the test when the other subjects were not

(B) Deciding that the test results are linked only to the amount of time each individual studied

(C) Deciding that half of the subjects may be very smart due to test results without the individual IQ test results

(D) Deciding that half of the subjects were highly motivated to succeed on the test due to the time they spent studying and the test results

(E) Deciding that half of the subjects were unmotivated to succeed on the test due to the time they spent studying and the test results

264. The tendency for early data about an individual to hold more weight than later data in forming impressions is called the

(A) fundamental attribution error

(B) primacy effect

(C) just-world hypothesis

(D) self-fulfilling prophecy

(E) first impression error

265. Schemata that put people of certain races, cultural backgrounds, or religious beliefs into negative categorizations are considered

(A) prejudices

(B) cognitions

(C) stereotypes

(D) beliefs

(E) none of the above

266. Cameron believed his skill allowed him to win the surf contest on Saturday, but he blamed the event organizers when he came in fifth in the overall water sports competition. Which error in attribution might Cameron have made?

(A) Fundamental attribution error

(B) Just-world hypothesis

(C) Defensive attribution error

(D) Cognitive bias

(E) Culturally biased attribution error

267. When an entire culture group was impacted by a natural disaster, many believed this group experienced a catastrophe because it was a group of "bad people." This assumption is a based on which attribution error?

(A) Fundamental attribution error
(B) Just-world hypothesis
(C) Culturally biased attribution error
(D) Defensive attribution error
(E) Judgment attribution error

268. Sometimes an individual will group all individuals of a different group (race, religion, class) as the same. This tendency is called

(A) out-group homogeneity
(B) in-group homogeneity
(C) out-group heterogeneity
(D) in-group heterogeneity
(E) both-group homogeneity

269. The discomfort caused by an inconsistency or contradiction between actions and attitudes is called

(A) persuasion
(B) cognitive dissonance
(C) schemata
(D) social influence
(E) self-fulfilling prophecy

270. Which of the following is NOT a direct factor in attitude development?

(A) Learning
(B) Family
(C) Peers
(D) Media
(E) IQ scores

271. Using attitudes to predict behavior is challenging with individuals who are or show

(A) low self-monitors
(B) high self-monitors
(C) low self-perception
(D) high self-perception
(E) vulnerability to persuasion

272. A Caucasian individual who believes strongly that his or her inability to get a decent job is based on affirmative action policies aimed at workplace diversity is demonstrating

(A) a self-fulfilling prophecy
(B) out-group homogeneity
(C) the frustration-aggression theory of prejudice
(D) attitudinal change
(E) cognitive dissonance

273. Which of the following is an example of a peripheral route to persuasion?

(A) An individual challenges his or her beliefs about a political candidate and explores the important social policies the candidate supports.
(B) An individual is persuaded to vote for a certain candidate after a debate because the candidate is attractive and charismatic.
(C) An individual holds strongly to his or her beliefs about a candidate based on the candidate's in-group status with the individual.
(D) An individual does careful Internet and library research to explore the arguments of the two candidates before choosing one.
(E) An individual evaluates the reasons for choosing a candidate and realizes that the original reasons were superficial, thus changing his or her choice.

274. Tina prides herself in living a healthy lifestyle and does so by eating healthy and exercising. At the same time, Tina is addicted to cigarettes. Her smoking habit causes discomfort for Tina. What is the state described by her conflicting attitudes and behaviors?

(A) Conformity
(B) Persuasion
(C) Self-fulfilling prophecy
(D) Self-perception theory
(E) Cognitive dissonance

275. According to the communication model of persuasion, which of the following is NOT a function of persuasion?

(A) Message
(B) Source
(C) Schema
(D) Medium
(E) Audience

276. Which of the following is NOT a strategy to reduce prejudices?
   (A) Uncovering underlying prejudices through empirical studies
   (B) Increasing exposure between groups among people with equal status
   (C) Recategorizing cognitive schemata
   (D) Increasing one-on-one contact across groups
   (E) Maintaining mindfulness of differences

277. High self-monitors act on _____, while low self-monitors act on _____.
   (A) expectations; attitudes
   (B) attitudes; expectations
   (C) expectations; prejudices
   (D) prejudices; expectations
   (E) self-perception; attitudes

278. A series of acts based on prejudicial attitudes that limits access to social capital and opportunities to a group of people and individual members of the group is considered
   (A) stereotyping
   (B) prejudice
   (C) aggression
   (D) discrimination
   (E) perception

Social Influence

279. The tendency of individuals to answer questions differently in front of others than they would on their own is a result of
   (A) obedience
   (B) truism
   (C) attitudes
   (D) cognitive dissonance
   (E) conformity

280. All of the following are forms of social influence EXCEPT
   (A) conformity
   (B) obedience
   (C) compliance
   (D) cognitive dissonance
   (E) group dynamics

281. Kristie's good friend is bossy and intimidating, so Kristie finds herself taking directions about what to do from her friend and doing things she would not otherwise do. What experience is Kristie having?

(A) Cooperation
(B) Obedience
(C) Compliance
(D) Conformity
(E) Groupthink

282. A fundraiser may ask for a very large donation with the expectation of getting a more moderate donation. This technique of getting compliance is called

(A) that's-not-all technique
(B) ingratiation technique
(C) foot-in-the-door technique
(D) door-in-the-face technique
(E) lowball procedure

283. A lack of action by a large group of people when they see an individual in need of help is called the

(A) polarization effect
(B) Hawthorne effect
(C) bystander effect
(D) social loafing
(E) cultural effect

284. The track coach at Millers High has students run the 50-meter dash against each other to track their best times. Which theory of group dynamics likely led to this decision?

(A) Social inhibition
(B) Social facilitation
(C) Groupthink
(D) Social loafing
(E) Polarization

285. Derek went with 10 of his friends to explore the damage caused by a tornado and was surprised to find himself looting some of the damaged stores. What experience did Derek likely encounter?

(A) Social inhibition
(B) Social loafing
(C) Mere presence effect
(D) Deindividuation
(E) Polarization

286. Conforming to group values and minimizing individual differences that can lead to faulty thinking and decision making is known as

(A) deindividuation
(B) social loafing
(C) groupthink
(D) group polarization
(E) social facilitation

287. In an effort to come to agreement on the case, members of the jury provide viewpoints that all can consider. Instead of bringing the jury members closer to a decision, the group becomes split and members move further from agreement. What process has happened in this case?

(A) Group polarization
(B) Groupthink
(C) Social facilitation
(D) Social inhibition
(E) Deindividuation

288. Students working on group projects who tend to do less work than they would on individual projects are experiencing

(A) polarization
(B) deindividuation
(C) groupthink
(D) social loafing
(E) social inhibition

289. Milgram's study involved students delivering progressively stronger electric shocks to actors because this was the instruction of the study leaders. This study provides data in the area of

(A) conformity
(B) obedience
(C) cultural norms
(D) attitudes
(E) cognitive dissonance

290. In which type of cultures is conformity likely to be higher?

(A) Individualist cultures
(B) Collectivist cultures
(C) Small subcultures
(D) Minority cultures
(E) Homogenous cultures

291. Which type of prosocial behavior includes helping without expectation of reward?

(A) Norm of reciprocity
(B) Individualist viewpoint
(C) Collectivist viewpoint
(D) Bystander effect
(E) Altruism

292. As the number of individuals in a group _____, the likelihood that an individual helps someone in distress _____.

(A) decreases; decreases
(B) increases; decreases
(C) increases; increases
(D) decreases; stays stable
(E) none of the above

293. Researchers must be aware that changes in productivity or behavior may exist purely due to the presence of the researcher. This phenomenon is called the

(A) Hawthorne effect
(B) bystander effect
(C) cultural effects
(D) halo effect
(E) polarization effect

294. An individual is stranded in her car on a busy highway, but not one of the passing cars stops to help. Which phenomena is likely at play?

(A) polarization effect
(B) Hawthorne effect
(C) bystander effect
(D) conformity
(E) cultural effects

295. Which of these factors provides clues to the way someone is feeling?

(A) What they say about their feelings
(B) Facial expressions
(C) Posture
(D) Overt behaviors
(E) All of the above

CHAPTER 9

Development

Development

296. Which two stages make up the prenatal period?

(A) Embryonic stage; fetal stage
(B) Fetal stage; uterine stage
(C) Embryonic stage; prenatal stage
(D) Fetal stage; prenatal stage
(E) Prenatal stage; perinatal stage

297. All of the following are functions of the placenta EXCEPT

(A) supply oxygen to fetus
(B) supply nutrients to fetus
(C) remove waste from uterine environment
(D) provide temperature regulation to fetus
(E) connect fetus to uterine wall

298. Which of the following correctly describes teratogens?

(A) Nutritional qualities that positively impact fetal development
(B) Nutritional deficits that negatively impact fetal development
(C) Biological substances within a uterine environment that negatively impact fetal development
(D) Environmental substances that negatively impact fetal development
(E) Environmental substances that positively impact fetal development

299. Which of the following is NOT a symptom of fetal alcohol syndrome?

(A) Heart defects
(B) Facial deformities
(C) Cognitive impairments
(D) Stunted growth
(E) Large head circumference

300. All of the following are reflexes that newborns typically express EXCEPT

(A) grasping
(B) sucking
(C) swallowing
(D) crying
(E) rooting

301. The patterns of behavior, emotion, and self-regulation that infants display are considered their

(A) personality
(B) temperament
(C) bonding
(D) attachment
(E) development

302. A young child who searches for his or her favorite toy under couches, in different rooms, and all around the house has clearly achieved which piece of cognitive awareness?

(A) Control mastery
(B) Conservation
(C) Object permanence
(D) Mental reasoning
(E) Abstract thinking

303. A child who sees a tiger stuffed animal for the first time and calls it a kitty is demonstrating

(A) egocentrism
(B) conservation
(C) accommodation
(D) object permanence
(E) assimilation

304. A baby with which type of temperament negatively reacts to new people and situations and is irritable?

(A) Shy child temperament
(B) Slow-to-warm-up temperament
(C) Difficult temperament
(D) Easy temperament
(E) Cheerful temperament

305. Which of the following is NOT an example of a teratogen?

(A) Alcohol
(B) X-ray exposure
(C) Prenatal vitamins
(D) Exposure to measles
(E) Air pollution

306. An infant who, when his or her cheek is touched, moves toward the stimulus and makes sucking motions is displaying the

(A) sucking reflex
(B) grasp reflex
(C) stepping reflex
(D) swallowing reflex
(E) rooting reflex

307. A baby with a slow-to-warm-up temperament displays

(A) high interest in new activities and experiences and high reactivity
(B) high interest in new activities and experiences and low reactivity
(C) low interest in new activities and experiences and low reactivity
(D) low interest in new activities and experiences and high reactivity
(E) low interest in new activities and experiences and no reactivity

308. During which of Piaget's stages of cognitive development does a child develop object permanence?

(A) Sensory-motor stage
(B) Preoperational stage
(C) Concrete operational stage
(D) Formal operational stage
(E) Postconventional stage

309. Which statement describes an individual in Kohlberg's preconventional stage of moral development?

(A) A 10-year-old cleans his room because he wants to.
(B) A 10-year-old cleans his room because it is the right thing to do.
(C) A 10-year-old refuses to clean his room to assert some autonomy.
(D) A 10-year-old cleans his room in order to be seen as a good boy.
(E) A 10-year-old cleans his room to earn time to play video games.

310. Which of Piaget's stages of cognitive development is characterized in part by egocentric thought?

(A) Sensory-motor stage
(B) Preoperational stage
(C) Concrete operational stage
(D) Formal operational stage
(E) Postconventional stage

311. _____ is to Piaget's formal operational stage as _____ is to Piaget's concrete operational stage.

(A) Concrete thinking; abstract thinking
(B) Abstract thinking; concrete thinking
(C) Language development; egocentric thinking
(D) Concrete thinking; egocentric thinking
(E) Abstract thinking; egocentric thinking

312. Which of the following is NOT a criticism of Piaget's theory?

(A) Lack of attention to social interactions
(B) Lack of attention to human diversity
(C) Possible variability from the distinct stages model
(D) Lack of empirical data
(E) Underrated infant cognitive capabilities

313. Which answer choice is NOT a limitation of a longitudinal study of development over time?

(A) High attrition
(B) High cost
(C) Time consuming
(D) Difficult to identify source of differences
(E) Elimination of participant group differences

Social Development

314. According to John Bowlby, what develops in parent-child relationships that are safe and where children feel adequately protected?

(A) Attachment
(B) Insecure attachment
(C) Secure base
(D) Internal working models
(E) Temperament

315. The tendency of some animal species to follow the first moving object they see shortly after birth and form an attachment is the process of

(A) orienting
(B) imprinting
(C) creating a secure base
(D) developing autonomy
(E) socializing

316. Charlie's father is quite strict, demands a great deal of obedience, and does not respond much to Charlie's accomplishments. Which parenting style does Charlie's father exhibit?

(A) Baumrind's parenting style
(B) Authoritarian parenting style
(C) Authoritative parenting style
(D) Permissive-indulgent parenting style
(E) Permissive-indifferent parenting style

317. Donna notices that her two-year-old plays side by side with her same-age cousins, but does not interact with them. What type of play is the two-year-old exhibiting?

(A) Solitary play
(B) Parallel play
(C) Cooperative play
(D) Onlooker play
(E) Role play

318. By what age should Andrea expect her newborn to say her first word?

(A) 3 years
(B) 2 years
(C) 18 months
(D) 1 year
(E) 6 months

319. According to Erikson's stages of psychosocial development, what is the first stage that involves feeding and caregiver attachment?

(A) Identity vs. role confusion
(B) Industry vs. inferiority
(C) Initiative vs. guilt
(D) Autonomy vs. shame and doubt
(E) Trust vs. mistrust

320. Which nonmedical factor plays a key part in cognitive functioning in later adulthood?

(A) Mental stimulation
(B) Biological predisposition for Alzheimer's disease
(C) Quality of caregivers
(D) Circulatory decline
(E) Social capital

321. Which three senses tend to decline as one reaches old age?

(A) Taste, smell, sight
(B) Taste, smell, hearing
(C) Smell, hearing, sight
(D) Taste, hearing, sight
(E) Smell, hearing, touch

322. When an infant gauges an adult's facial expressions to gain data about his or her surroundings, what is the infant engaging in?

(A) Mirroring
(B) Imitating
(C) Interacting
(D) Social referencing
(E) Face recognition

323. A permissive-indifferent parenting style is to _____ children
as a permissive-indulgent parenting style is to _____ children.

   (A) dependent; impulsive
   (B) impulsive; dependent
   (C) independent; impulsive
   (D) dependent; independent
   (E) impulsive; independent

324. All of the following occur at approximately three years of age EXCEPT

   (A) language with short sentences
   (B) cooperative play
   (C) gender identity
   (D) early preoperational stage
   (E) menarche

325. Studies show that the impact of the initial arrival of babies into
a marriage is

   (A) increased marital satisfaction
   (B) decreased marital satisfaction
   (C) stable marital satisfaction
   (D) increased sexual drive
   (E) decreased sexual drive

326. Which of the following is NOT one of Kübler-Ross's stages of dying?

   (A) Anger
   (B) Denial
   (C) Bargaining
   (D) Stress
   (E) Acceptance

327. Which of Erikson's stages of psychosocial development occurs during
adolescence and includes social relationships as a key factor?

   (A) Industry versus inferiority
   (B) Identity versus role confusion
   (C) Intimacy versus isolation
   (D) Generativity versus stagnation
   (E) Ego integrity versus despair

328. Which parenting style is associated with children who are socially responsible and self-sufficient?

(A) Authoritative parenting
(B) Authoritarian parenting
(C) Permissive-indulgent parenting
(D) Permissive-independent parenting
(E) Disengaged parenting

329. Developing peer relationships impacts all of these arenas EXCEPT

(A) level of social support
(B) level of emotional support
(C) temperament
(D) problem-solving abilities
(E) positive play experiences

330. Primary sexual characteristic is to _____ as secondary sexual characteristic is to _____.

(A) pubic hair growth; breast development
(B) breast development; pubic hair growth
(C) testes growth; facial hair growth
(D) facial hair growth; testes growth
(E) beginning of menstruation; testes growth

331. Increased insecurities related to self-esteem and self-image may lead to increased levels of _____ in adolescents.

(A) depression
(B) anxiety
(C) personality disorders
(D) social phobia
(E) panic attacks

332. Which of the following is NOT expected in the adolescent experience?

(A) Impulsivity
(B) Lack of feelings of vulnerability
(C) Belief that they are central focus
(D) Formation of bonds exclusively with caregivers
(E) Attraction to very exciting stimuli

333. Industry versus inferiority is to _____ as generativity versus stagnation is to _____.

   (A) school aged; preschool
   (B) preschool; school aged
   (C) school aged; middle aged
   (D) middle aged; school aged
   (E) preschool; middle aged

CHAPTER 10

Personality

Personality

334. All of the following are included in the Big Five personality dimensions EXCEPT

(A) extroversion
(B) openness
(C) conscientiousness
(D) cognition
(E) neuroticism

335. Peter demonstrates similar patterns of behaving, feeling, and thinking in all different circumstances of his life. What are these similar patterns called?

(A) States
(B) Traits
(C) Factors
(D) Genetics
(E) Learning

336. The idea that psychological factors exist outside of consciousness and a focus on early childhood experiences is a contribution of

(A) humanistic theory
(B) cognitive-social learning theory
(C) psychodynamic theory
(D) positive psychology theory
(E) Big Five dimensions

337. According to Freudian theory, an individual who is guided only by pleasure, has no internalized social rules of behavior, and has little ability to balance the id with reality demonstrates an

(A) overdeveloped ego
(B) overdeveloped id
(C) overdeveloped superego
(D) underdeveloped superego
(E) underdeveloped id

338. The concept of the collective unconscious comes from

(A) humanistic theory
(B) psychoanalytic theory
(C) positive psychology
(D) social-cognitive theory
(E) Jungian theory

339. All of the following are patterns of attachment EXCEPT

(A) confused
(B) disorganized
(C) secure
(D) anxious resistant
(E) anxious avoidant

340. Who is responsible for the theory that individuals develop a secure sense of identity through mastering stages such as trust versus mistrust and identity versus role confusion?

(A) Karen Horney
(B) Sigmund Freud
(C) Erik Erikson
(D) Carl Rogers
(E) Carl Jung

341. The self-actualizing tendency is one that encourages people to

(A) create relationships
(B) reach their potential
(C) minimize anxiety
(D) maximize superego
(E) create autonomy

342. A theory of psychological functioning that steers away from psychopathology and the origins of problems is called
(A) Jungian theory
(B) psychodynamic theory
(C) positive psychology
(D) self psychology
(E) ego psychology

343. Which of the following is characteristic of psychodynamic theory?
(A) Mental representations of ourselves, sometimes unconscious, inform our relationships.
(B) All behavior is driven only by drives.
(C) Therapeutic focus is only on the present and the future.
(D) Individuals are driven to grow and function at higher levels.
(E) Behavior is guided by thought, previous experiences, and learning.

344. According to Freud, which structure of personality acts as a guide to moral behavior?
(A) Id
(B) Ego
(C) Superego
(D) Defense
(E) Repression

345. The ＿＿＿＿＿＿＿ mediates between the ＿＿＿＿＿＿＿ and ＿＿＿＿＿＿＿.
(A) id; ego; superego
(B) ego; id; superego
(C) superego; id; ego
(D) superego; ego; id
(E) ego; superego; ego

346. The belief of humans as naturally self-actualizing beings, the belief in human good, and the belief in unconditional positive regard are all tenets of which theory?
(A) Psychodynamic theory
(B) Attachment theory
(C) Drive theories
(D) Behaviorism
(E) Humanism

347. Which stage of psychosexual development of Freudian theory is characterized by no interest in the opposite sex?

(A) Oral stage
(B) Anal stage
(C) Phallic stage
(D) Latency stage
(E) Genital stage

348. According to Freudian theory, what is the purpose of defense mechanisms?

(A) To protect the individual from the criticism of others
(B) To mediate between the id and the superego
(C) To protect the individual from the anxiety caused by the inability to satisfy the id while maintaining standards of the superego
(D) To defend the individual from dealing with his or her sexual drives
(E) To defend the individual from his or her id-related pleasure by creating an overfunctioning superego

349. An individual whose ego does not live up to the expectations or moral principles of the superego may experience

(A) pride
(B) guilt
(C) depression
(D) joy
(E) self-importance

350. Which defense mechanism is characterized by keeping painful thoughts or memories outside of the conscious experience?

(A) Regression
(B) Repression
(C) Projection
(D) Identification
(E) Denial

351. Erikson is to _____ as Rogers is to _____.

(A) eight stages of development; psychosexual development
(B) parent-child relationship quality; self-actualization
(C) self-actualization; parent-child relationship quality
(D) personal and collective unconscious; self-actualization
(E) self-actualization; personal and collective unconscious

352. According to Horney, what is the main motivating force for individuals?

(A) Libido
(B) Relationships
(C) Anxiety
(D) Social mores
(E) Perfection

353. According to Jung, which type of individual is mainly concerned with his or her private internal world?

(A) Introvert
(B) Extrovert
(C) Rational
(D) Irrational
(E) Neurotic

354. An individual who expresses outward disdain for homosexuality but who actually has internal homosexual thoughts is displaying

(A) sublimation
(B) reaction formation
(C) displacement
(D) intellectualization
(E) projection

355. According to Freudian theory, boys experience _____ and girls experience _____.

(A) Oedipal complex; penis envy
(B) Oedipal complex; oral fixation
(C) Electra complex; Oedipal complex
(D) Electra complex; oral fixation
(E) Oedipal complex; Electra complex

356. All of the following are criticisms of psychodynamic theories EXCEPT

(A) lack of empirical evidence
(B) subjectivity
(C) lack of evidence of importance of relationships
(D) culture bound
(E) gender biased

357. The archetypes of the anima and animus are part of the

    (A) personal unconscious
    (B) collective archetypes
    (C) collective unconscious
    (D) persona
    (E) phenomenology

358. What type of theories are object relations and ego psychology?

    (A) Humanistic theories
    (B) Jungian theories
    (C) Social-cognitive theories
    (D) Psychodynamic theories
    (E) Behavioral theories

359. The social-cognitive approach to personality includes all of the following factors EXCEPT

    (A) cognitions
    (B) past experiences
    (C) the unconscious
    (D) learning
    (E) experience in the social universe

360. An individual who demonstrates a belief that events are a result of one's own actions and that one has control over outcomes has a strong

    (A) external locus of control
    (B) internal locus of control
    (C) disbelief in self-efficacy
    (D) set of personal constructs
    (E) sense of expectancies

361. Which contribution do cognitive-social approaches bring to the field of psychology regarding psychological treatments?

    (A) Treatment without time limits
    (B) Attention on motivation
    (C) Projective personality assessment
    (D) Integration of cognitions and the unconscious
    (E) Scientifically testable

362. The Minnesota Multiphasic Personality Inventory (MMPI-2) is an example of which type of personality assessment?

(A) Unstructured interview
(B) Semistructured interview
(C) Self-report objective
(D) Projective self-report test
(E) Direct observation

363. Bandura's concept of behaviors being influenced by internal expectations is called

(A) locus of control
(B) cognitive behavioral therapy
(C) self-efficacy
(D) social learning
(E) self-determination

364. A psychologist sees a client who reports a belief that he can do nothing to change his difficult circumstances and believes that others always determine his fate. Which quality does this client demonstrate?

(A) Low self-esteem
(B) High self-esteem
(C) Internal locus of control
(D) External locus of control
(E) Positive attributional style

365. Which perspective on personality has a focus on an individual's experiences, thoughts and feelings about the experiences, and the amount of control the individual has about those experiences?

(A) Humanistic approach
(B) Cognitive-social approach
(C) Cognitive behavioral therapy
(D) Psychodynamic approach
(E) Rogerian approach

366. Which assessment uses interpretations of inkblots to assess personality and emotional functioning?

(A) MMPI
(B) TAT
(C) IQ test
(D) Rorschach test
(E) SCID

367. Which of the following is NOT a factor of the Big Five personality trait of neuroticism?

(A) Impulse control
(B) Agreeableness
(C) Anxiety
(D) Achievement orientation
(E) Emotional stability

CHAPTER 11

Psychopathology

Psychopathology

368. The historical somatogenic hypothesis of mental disorders is most similar to which modern-day model of causes of psychological disorders?

(A) Psychoanalytic model
(B) Cognitive behavioral model
(C) Diathesis-stress model
(D) Biological model
(E) Systems theory

369. Patient reports are to _____ as clinician observations are to _____.

(A) signs; symptoms
(B) symptoms; signs
(C) signs; affect
(D) affect; symptoms
(E) behaviors; symptoms

370. Which of the following is NOT a criticism of the DSM and psychological diagnosis?

(A) Reinforcing stigma
(B) Labeling
(C) Disease model
(D) Treatment guidance
(E) Generic symptom description

371. The definition of mental disorders that comes from the *Diagnostic and Statistical Manual of Mental Disorders* includes all of the following aspects EXCEPT

(A) behavioral or psychological distress
(B) increased risk of suffering
(C) not a result of bereavement
(D) of biological origin
(E) not a culturally accepted response to a stressor

372. Which of the following individuals is experiencing compulsions?

(A) A young woman feels shortness of breath and a racing heart in a crowd.
(B) A young woman thinks constantly about dirt and germs.
(C) A young woman sees images that other people do not see.
(D) A young woman feels intense cravings for a particular substance.
(E) A young woman washes her hands more than 50 times a day to avoid germs.

373. Which psychological disorder is associated with symptoms of avoidance, hyperarousal, and re-experiencing?

(A) Acute stress disorder
(B) Posttraumatic stress disorder
(C) Substance abuse disorder
(D) Substance dependence
(E) Schizophrenia

374. A mental disorder characterized by frequent worry about many things that drifts from one thing to the next is known as

(A) generalized anxiety disorder
(B) panic disorder
(C) specific phobia
(D) agoraphobia
(E) obsessive-compulsive disorder

375. Terry's roommate has been barely sleeping for days, talking quite quickly, and having grandiose thoughts about himself and his abilities. He also has spent thousands of dollars in a few days. What is Terry's roommate likely experiencing?

(A) Depression
(B) Insomnia
(C) Mania
(D) Psychosis
(E) Obsessions

376. All of the following are symptoms of depression EXCEPT

(A) excessive sadness
(B) decreased interest in pleasurable activities
(C) euphoric feelings
(D) excessive guilt
(E) fatigue

377. Which description is an example of the diathesis-stress model of psychological disorders?

(A) A teenaged boy has an organic brain disorder leading to psychosis.
(B) A teenaged boy has no history of psychological disorders but has a psychotic break after his parents' divorce.
(C) A teenaged boy experiments with drugs and has a psychotic break after the experimentation.
(D) A teenaged boy has unconscious conflicts related to early relationships, leading to his current depression.
(E) A teenaged boy believes himself to be "stupid"; therefore, he is not doing well in school and is depressed.

378. When making a DSM diagnosis, on which axis would one assess social or environmental problems?

(A) Axis I
(B) Axis II
(C) Axis III
(D) Axis IV
(E) Axis V

379. What is the likely diagnosis for an individual who experiences sadness, hopelessness, and generally low mood as well as mood states of euphoria, racing thoughts, and pressured speech?

(A) Depression
(B) Major depressive disorder
(C) Panic disorder
(D) Schizophrenia
(E) Bipolar disorder

380. Dylan experiences intense worry and discomfort about many things in his life, and this worry and discomfort limits his functioning. Which diagnostic category most likely characterizes Dylan's experience?

(A) Mood disorder
(B) Substance abuse disorder
(C) Anxiety disorder
(D) Personality disorder
(E) Thought disorder

381. Which psychological symptom is characterized by frequent and recurrent disturbing thoughts?

(A) Compulsions
(B) Panic attacks
(C) Hypomania
(D) Obsessions
(E) Pressured speech

382. A man who has negative automatic thoughts about himself, feels he has no value or control of the future, and, therefore, does not try to help himself in the world, may be at risk for depression due to his

(A) self-esteem
(B) cognitive distortions
(C) beliefs
(D) genetic factors
(E) all-or-nothing thinking

383. Which factor is associated with the fact that men are more likely to complete suicide attempts?

(A) Lethality of methods
(B) Mental disorder
(C) Increased likelihood of hospitalization
(D) Longevity of suffering
(E) Number of attempts

384. Which tool might a clinician use to assess the diagnostic category of an individual?

(A) MMPI
(B) BDI
(C) SCID
(D) DSM-IV-TR
(E) ICD-9

385. Which model of the causes of psychological disorders is inclusive of biological, social, and psychological risk factors?

(A) Psychoanalytical model
(B) Diathesis-stress model
(C) Systems theory
(D) Learning model
(E) Ecological model

386. After an intake, a psychologist makes the following notes: "patient showed little eye contact, had physical rigidity, and had a blunted affect." What do these notes describe?

(A) Patient's symptoms
(B) Patient's diagnosis
(C) Patient's signs
(D) Psychologist's impressions
(E) Psychologist's theoretical background

387. On which axis of a five-axes diagnosis would you list current psychological diagnoses, including generalized anxiety disorder or major depressive disorder?

(A) Axis I
(B) Axis II
(C) Axis III
(D) Axis IV
(E) Axis V

388. What term may be used by a legal expert, not a psychologist, to describe one who is mentally disturbed and, therefore, not responsible for his or her actions?

(A) Mentally ill
(B) Psychotic
(C) Insane
(D) Schizophrenic
(E) Diagnosable

389. Which mood disorder is characterized by a long period of a low-level depressed mood?

(A) Major depressive disorder
(B) Dysthymia
(C) Bipolar disorder
(D) Hypomania
(E) Mania

390. Which of the following are cognitive symptoms of depression?

(A) Feelings of hopelessness and guilt
(B) Fatigue and loss of appetite
(C) Concentration and memory impairment
(D) Depressed mood and lack of interest in pleasurable activities
(E) Low libido and insomnia

391. Which mental disorder is most commonly associated with successful suicide?

(A) Major depression
(B) Schizophrenia
(C) Panic disorder
(D) Obsessive compulsive disorder
(E) Bipolar disorder

392. Which neurotransmitter is most closely associated with depression?

(A) Dopamine
(B) Serotonin
(C) Norepinephrine
(D) GABA
(E) Glutamate

393. An individual who has a false belief that he or she is being followed by the FBI is experiencing a(n)

(A) delusion
(B) hallucination
(C) paranoia
(D) compulsion
(E) obsession

394. Which neurotransmitter is associated with psychosis and, therefore, schizophrenia?

  (A) Serotonin
  (B) GABA
  (C) Dopamine
  (D) Norepinephrine
  (E) Epinephrine

395. Which of the following is NOT a subtype of schizophrenia?

  (A) Paranoid schizophrenia
  (B) Catatonic schizophrenia
  (C) Recurrent schizophrenia
  (D) Undifferentiated schizophrenia
  (E) Disorganized schizophrenia

396. Schizoid, antisocial, and borderline are examples of

  (A) psychological symptoms
  (B) personality disorders
  (C) patterns of relating
  (D) signs of schizophrenia
  (E) developmental disorders

397. Which of the following is NOT a risk factor for mood disorders?

  (A) Psychological risks
  (B) Genetic predisposition
  (C) Social stigma on seeking help
  (D) Social supports
  (E) Neurobiological factors

398. Which category of mental disorders is the most common in the United States?

  (A) Mood disorders
  (B) Anxiety disorders
  (C) Thought disorders
  (D) Personality disorders
  (E) Substance abuse disorders

399. Which of the following are considered positive symptoms of schizophrenia?

(A) Anhedonia and social withdrawal
(B) Hallucinations and social withdrawal
(C) Catatonia and social withdrawal
(D) Catatonia and anhedonia
(E) Hallucinations and delusions

400. Which disorder diagnosed in childhood is characterized by marked deficiencies in behavior, communication, and socialization?

(A) Mental retardation
(B) Attention-deficit/hyperactivity disorder
(C) Enuresis
(D) Autism
(E) Anorexia nervosa

401. A young adult female finds her mind wandering while studying, procrastinates on all schoolwork, is somewhat impulsive, and has been told since childhood that she does not perform to her potential. What may she be experiencing?

(A) Attention-deficit/hyperactivity disorder
(B) Generalized anxiety disorder
(C) Panic disorder
(D) Autism
(E) Learning disorder

402. Claire has a cognitive schema that the world is a dangerous place and, therefore, experiences panic attacks whenever she leaves the house. In order to limit the panic attacks, Claire now stays in her home and family members take care of her food needs. Which mental disorder is Claire likely experiencing?

(A) Specific phobia
(B) Panic disorder with agoraphobia
(C) Panic disorder without agoraphobia
(D) Obsessive compulsive disorder
(E) Generalized anxiety disorder

403. All of the following are symptoms of posttraumatic stress disorder EXCEPT

   (A) flashbacks
   (B) compulsions
   (C) dissociation
   (D) nightmares
   (E) rapid heartbeat when reminded of stressor

404. Which disorder that involves the emergence of distinctly different personalities in one person has been portrayed in the media and at times misdiagnosed by therapists?

   (A) Borderline personality disorder
   (B) Dissociative identity disorder
   (C) Posttraumatic stress disorder
   (D) Dissociative fugue
   (E) Schizophrenia

405. An individual who experiences a physical symptom with no physical cause may be experiencing a(n)

   (A) somatoform disorder
   (B) thought disorder
   (C) mood disorder
   (D) developmental disorder
   (E) adjustment disorder

406. Marcia refuses to ride elevators, only takes stairs or escalators, and avoids doctors or any other appointments that are not accessible by stairs or escalators. What is Marcia's most likely diagnosis?

   (A) Generalized anxiety disorder
   (B) Agoraphobia
   (C) Social phobia
   (D) Specific phobia
   (E) Panic disorder

407. Obsessions are to _____ as compulsions are to _____.

   (A) feelings; behaviors
   (B) behaviors; feelings
   (C) thoughts; behaviors
   (D) behaviors; thoughts
   (E) thoughts; feelings

408. Which psychological disorder may be a result of classical conditioning?

(A) Generalized anxiety disorder
(B) Posttraumatic stress disorder
(C) Bipolar disorder
(D) Major depressive disorder
(E) Phobias

409. An individual who undergoes a break from reality is experiencing

(A) neurosis
(B) psychosis
(C) paranoia
(D) delusions
(E) schizophrenia

410. Which disorder is characterized by binge eating and compensatory behaviors?

(A) Body dysmorphic disorder
(B) Anorexia nervosa
(C) Bulimia nervosa
(D) Binge eating disorder
(E) Compulsive overeating

411. Which disorders may be associated with trauma, typically involve memory loss, and involve an unconscious process of psychologically distancing oneself from current reality?

(A) Fugue disorders
(B) Dissociative disorders
(C) Personality disorders
(D) Amnesic disorders
(E) Mood disorders

412. Which statement is true about schizophrenia?

(A) The negative symptoms are more difficult to identify and treat.
(B) The positive symptoms are more difficult to identify and treat.
(C) The organic symptoms are more difficult to identify and treat.
(D) All of the symptoms are treated with typical or atypical antipsychotics.
(E) Antipsychotic medications have few side effects.

413. Betty visits doctors weekly and is constantly concerned that she is dying. She has symptoms of many different ailments, none of which are found by the medical professionals. Which type of disorder is Betty likely experiencing?

(A) Conversion disorder
(B) Somatoform disorder
(C) Substance abuse disorder
(D) Thought disorder
(E) Anxiety disorder

414. Which type of mental disorder results in pervasive patterns of thinking and behaving that lead to distress in the individual or in relating with others?

(A) Disorder of childhood
(B) Developmental disorder
(C) Personality disorder
(D) Learning disorder
(E) Thought disorder

415. Which disorder impacts children and adults with regard to impulsiveness, inattention, and hyperactivity?

(A) ADHD
(B) PDD
(C) Borderline personality disorder
(D) Bipolar disorder
(E) Depression

416. A five-year-old boy who does not speak, makes no eye contact, displays interest in repetitive tasks like moving a truck back and forth, and is very upset by changes in his sensory environment may be experiencing which mental disorder?

(A) Mental retardation
(B) Panic disorder
(C) Autism
(D) Conduct disorder
(E) Attention deficit disorder

417. According to twin studies on schizophrenia, schizophrenia appears to

(A) cause decreased serotonin in the synaptic cleft
(B) have no impact on brain structures
(C) have a genetic link
(D) cause increased firing of neurons
(E) have no genetic link

418. Which perspective on somatoform disorders considers the benefits that an individual gets from being in the sick role?

(A) Biological perspective
(B) Cognitive-behavioral perspective
(C) Psychodynamic perspective
(D) Freudian perspective
(E) Systems perspective

419. Which of the following is NOT true about anorexia nervosa?

(A) It is more common in females.
(B) It is culturally determined.
(C) It is characterized by binging and purging.
(D) It is characterized by refusal to maintain body weight.
(E) It is more common in individuals with genetically related relatives with the disorder.

420. The fact that an underacting thyroid gland can lead to depressed symptoms supports which model of psychological disorders?

(A) Cognitive-behavioral model
(B) Psychoanalytic model
(C) Diathesis-stress model
(D) Biopsychosocial model
(E) Biological model

421. What category of psychological disorders is characterized by sexual attraction to unconventional objects or circumstances?

(A) Sexual arousal disorders
(B) Orgasmic disorders
(C) Sexual desire disorders
(D) Paraphilias
(E) Erectile disorders

422. Brett, a 20-year-old man, is in prison for violent crimes against others and has been arrested frequently for breaking the law. But he is also quite charming. He reports torturing animals as a child and frequent difficulties in school. Which psychological disorder is Brett likely experiencing?

(A) Schizophrenia
(B) Bipolar disorder
(C) Personality disorder
(D) Generalized anxiety disorder
(E) Dissociative disorder

CHAPTER 12

Treatment of Mental Disorders

Psychological Treatments

423. Which type of professional does NOT provide psychological treatment for mental disorders?

(A) Clinical psychologist
(B) Psychiatrist
(C) Clinical social worker
(D) Internist
(E) Marriage and family counselor

424. All of the following conditions may influence someone to seek psychological treatment EXCEPT

(A) a diagnosable mental disorder
(B) symptoms of a mental disorder, but not a full diagnosis
(C) relationship problems
(D) literacy issues
(E) difficulty with decision making

425. Regardless of theoretical orientation, it is critical that a mental health therapist have

(A) a license to practice
(B) an educational transcript
(C) cultural competence
(D) political awareness
(E) experience as a client

426. Mary sees her therapist as a mother figure and frequently responds to her therapist as she responded to her mother in her teens. What is Mary's experience of her therapist called?

(A) Projection
(B) Transference
(C) Psychodynamics
(D) Free association
(E) Symptom

427. All of the following are considered insight-oriented therapies EXCEPT

(A) brief psychodynamic psychotherapy
(B) psychoanalysis
(C) gestalt therapy
(D) interpersonal therapy
(E) exposure therapy

428. Fritz Perls is associated with which type of therapy?

(A) Gestalt therapy
(B) Client-centered therapy
(C) Psychoanalysis
(D) Cognitive-behavioral therapy
(E) Group therapy

429. Which type of psychotherapy includes active listening and unconditional positive regard?

(A) Psychoanalysis
(B) Rational emotive therapy
(C) Client-centered therapy
(D) Cognitive therapy
(E) Gestalt therapy

430. Which two types of therapies target irrational beliefs and negative self-thinking for interventions?

(A) Cognitive therapy and exposure therapy
(B) Cognitive therapy and rational emotive therapy
(C) Exposure therapy and interpersonal therapy
(D) Rational emotive therapy and extinction
(E) Interpersonal therapy and extinction

431. Which type of professional provides both psychological and biological interventions for mental disorders?

(A) Marriage and family counselor
(B) Clinical social worker
(C) Psychiatrist
(D) Clinical psychologist
(E) Pastoral counselor

432. All of the following techniques are based in classical conditioning EXCEPT

(A) systematic desensitization
(B) token economy
(C) flooding
(D) aversive conditioning
(E) extinction

433. Cognitive therapy is to _____ as client-centered therapy is to _____.

(A) Freud; Rogers
(B) Rogers; Freud
(C) Freud; Beck
(D) Rogers; Beck
(E) Beck; Rogers

434. All of the following describe circumstances in which psychological treatment is appropriate EXCEPT

(A) Alison seeks treatment for a recurrent major depressive disorder
(B) Alison seeks treatment to gain insight about her role in relationships
(C) Alison seeks treatment related to her diet to manage an iron deficiency
(D) Alison seeks treatment related to high workplace stress
(E) Alison seeks treatment after witnessing a traumatic event

435. In which approach to psychotherapy does the therapist remain neutral?

(A) Psychoanalysis
(B) Psychodynamic psychotherapy
(C) Interpersonal therapy
(D) Cognitive behavioral psychotherapy
(E) Gestalt therapy

436. Andrea has an intense fear of public speaking. During her course of therapy, Andrea makes a list of her fears related to public speaking, ordering them from the least of her fears to her worst fear. She will work through this list with her therapist. Which type of psychotherapy is Andrea likely seeking?

(A) Behavioral therapy
(B) Exposure therapy
(C) Flooding
(D) Psychodynamic therapy
(E) Client-centered therapy

437. A therapist who works with a client about unconscious conflicts and defenses, interpersonal relationships, and present and past experiences likely practices which type of psychotherapy?

(A) Client-centered therapy
(B) Behavioral therapy
(C) Humanistic therapy
(D) Psychodynamic therapy
(E) Exposure therapy

438. According to psychotherapy research, which type of psychotherapy is the most effective most of the time?

(A) Cognitive therapy
(B) Psychodynamic therapy
(C) Behavioral therapy
(D) Client-centered therapy
(E) None of the above

439. Assigning feelings related to childhood authority figures to the therapist is called

(A) transference
(B) projection
(C) introjection
(D) countertransference
(E) defenses

440. Which category of psychotherapy is client-centered therapy?
- (A) Behavioral therapies
- (B) Humanistic therapies
- (C) Psychoanalytic therapies
- (D) Cognitive therapies
- (E) Family therapies

441. A client who has frequent problems in relationships and communication may benefit from which type of time-limited psychotherapy focused on interpersonal deficits, loss, role transitions, and role disputes?
- (A) Client-centered psychotherapy
- (B) Cognitive therapy
- (C) Exposure therapy
- (D) Interpersonal therapy
- (E) Gestalt therapy

442. The behavioral technique of driving through tunnels repeatedly to help someone dispel a fear of bridges is known as
- (A) exposure therapy
- (B) systematic desensitization
- (C) flooding
- (D) extinction
- (E) token economy

443. Which type of therapy is rooted in the idea that activating events are influenced by an individual's beliefs, which then influence consequences?
- (A) Interpersonal therapy
- (B) Cognitive therapy
- (C) Rational emotive therapy
- (D) Gestalt therapy
- (E) Psychodynamic therapy

444. A depressed man believes he is not worthy of finding a partner and not competent at his job. He also is hopeless about the future. Which type of therapy may he benefit from that focuses on his thoughts and beliefs?
- (A) Psychoanalytic therapy
- (B) Exposure therapy
- (C) Client-centered therapy
- (D) Interpersonal therapy
- (E) Cognitive therapy

445. In a residential treatment facility for adolescents, the adolescents receive rewards at the end of each day based on their behaviors. The rewards can be traded for trinkets or other items. What type of therapy does this example describe?

(A) Exposure therapy
(B) Flooding
(C) Extinction
(D) Token economy
(E) Contingency management

446. Courtney is working in psychotherapy on better integrating the parts of herself into a whole. At one point, she engaged in an empty chair experiment. Which modality of psychotherapy is Courtney likely engaged in?

(A) Psychoanalysis
(B) Client-centered therapy
(C) Gestalt therapy
(D) Exposure therapy
(E) Cognitive therapy

447. Which approach does a family therapist typically take when looking at the problems of a family?

(A) The problems are a result of one family member.
(B) The problems are a result of each family member.
(C) The problems are a result of external systems the family has access to.
(D) The problems are a result of the entire family system.
(E) The problems are a result of the children's behaviors.

448. A therapist who demonstrates to a client a way of thinking that does NOT involve a cognitive distortion of catastrophizing is performing which behavioral intervention?

(A) Flooding
(B) Virtual reality exposure
(C) Token economy
(D) Modeling
(E) Transference

449. Which of the following describes the basic tenet of behavioral therapies?

(A) Behavior is based on unconscious drives.

(B) Behavior is learned.

(C) Behavior is based on feelings of self.

(D) Behavior is based in biological roots.

(E) None of the above

450. On an inpatient psychiatric unit, patients are given bonus points for attending groups. Bonus points are traded for candy and other items. Which therapeutic technique is being used?

(A) Token economy

(B) Active listening

(C) Transference

(D) Countertransference

(E) Contingency management

451. The therapist is generally neutral in _____, whereas the therapist is quite active in _____.

(A) gestalt therapy; psychodynamic psychotherapy

(B) cognitive therapy; psychoanalysis

(C) psychodynamic psychotherapy; psychoanalysis

(D) cognitive therapy; gestalt therapy

(E) psychoanalysis; gestalt therapy

452. Ellis is to _____ as Beck is to _____.

(A) rational emotive therapy; cognitive therapy

(B) cognitive therapy; rational emotive therapy

(C) rational emotive therapy; behavioral therapy

(D) behavioral therapy; rational emotive therapy

(E) cognitive therapy; psychodynamic therapy

453. Which of the following psychotherapies is NOT considered an insight-oriented approach?

(A) Psychodynamic psychotherapy

(B) Psychoanalysis

(C) Gestalt therapy

(D) Systematic desensitization

(E) Client-centered therapy

454. Which type of group therapy is Alcoholics Anonymous?

(A) Psychotherapy group
(B) Psychoeducation group
(C) Self-help group
(D) Family therapy
(E) Music therapy

455. What is the most common theoretical orientation of therapists in this decade?

(A) Psychoanalysis
(B) Rational emotive therapy
(C) Client-centered therapy
(D) Cognitive therapy
(E) Eclectic approaches to therapy

456. What is a benefit of using a manualized psychotherapy intervention?

(A) It is more beneficial to patients.
(B) It lends itself to research.
(C) It provides patients with homework.
(D) It is difficult to learn.
(E) It is generally more effective.

Biomedical Treatments

457. What term is used to describe all of the classes of medication that are used to treat mental disorders or symptoms of mental disorders?

(A) Antidepressants
(B) Psychotropics
(C) Antipsychotics
(D) Narcotics
(E) Benzodiazepines

458. Which type of treatment provider is involved in prescribing medication for mental disorders?

(A) Clinical social worker
(B) Clinical psychologist
(C) School psychologist
(D) Psychiatrist
(E) Professional counselor

459. Which type of medication acts by blocking dopamine receptors to treat the positive symptoms of schizophrenia?

(A) Antidepressants
(B) Benzodiazepines
(C) Psychostimulants
(D) MAOIs
(E) Antipsychotics

460. Fluoxetine acts to prevent the reuptake of serotonin, leaving more serotonin in the synapse. Which type of medication is fluoxetine?

(A) TCA
(B) MAOI
(C) SSRI
(D) SNRI
(E) Placebo

461. Which naturally occurring substance is used to treat bipolar disorder?

(A) Saint-John's-wort
(B) Lithium
(C) Depakote
(D) Cannabis
(E) Folic acid

462. What is a common side effect of electroconvulsive therapy?

(A) Weight gain
(B) Loss of libido
(C) Memory loss
(D) Dry mouth
(E) Tardive dyskinesia

463. What is a common side effect of psychostimulants?

(A) Loss of libido
(B) Loss of appetite
(C) Loss of ability to feel pleasure
(D) Loss of concentration
(E) Memory loss

464. The "thorazine shuffle" and tardive dyskinesia are side effects of

   (A) antidepressants
   (B) antipsychotics
   (C) atypical antipsychotics
   (D) anxiolytics
   (E) mood stabilizers

465. Which statement is NOT true of benzodiazepines?

   (A) One type of benzodiazepine is Valium.
   (B) They are used to minimize anxiety.
   (C) They stimulate the nervous system.
   (D) They have the potential for addiction.
   (E) Taking benzodiazepines and using alcohol can be a dangerous combination.

466. Which type of medication might be prescribed to someone with bipolar disorder?

   (A) An antipsychotic
   (B) An anxiolytic
   (C) A mood stabilizer
   (D) An antidepressant
   (E) A psychostimulant

467. Which biomedical treatment was found to severely impair cognitive functioning and self-regulation, causing it to be rarely practiced in present-day medicine?

   (A) Prefrontal lobotomy
   (B) Shock therapy
   (C) Transcranial magnetic stimulation
   (D) Psychopharmacology
   (E) Vagal nerve stimulation

468. A child with ADHD may be prescribed which type of medication?

   (A) An antidepressant
   (B) An anxiolytic
   (C) An antipsychotic
   (D) A psychostimulant
   (E) A benzodiazepine

469. What is one of the main benefits of the second generation, atypical antipsychotic medication?

(A) They cause weight loss.
(B) They target both negative and positive symptoms of schizophrenia.
(C) They eliminate hallucinations associated with schizophrenia.
(D) They eliminate delusions associated with schizophrenia.
(E) They have no side effects.

470. The social policy that moved many patients with mental disorders from hospitals into the community was called

(A) community mental health
(B) National Mental Health Act
(C) deinstitutionalization
(D) managed care
(E) health care reform

471. MAOIs, TCAs, SSRIs, and SNRIs are examples of which category of medications?

(A) Atypical antipsychotics
(B) Antipsychotics
(C) Anxiolytics
(D) Antidepressants
(E) Psychostimulants

472. What type of biomedical intervention may be used after many medications and therapies have been proven ineffective, and the individual has serious depressed symptoms and thoughts of suicide?

(A) Intensive outpatient treatment
(B) Electroconvulsive therapy
(C) Group therapy
(D) Hypnosis
(E) Light box treatment

473. Which type of medication might be prescribed to someone with recurring panic attacks?

(A) Antidepressant
(B) Antipsychotic
(C) Mood stabilizer
(D) Psychostimulant
(E) Anxiolytic

474. Which class of medications is used to treat both bipolar disorder and schizophrenia?

(A) SSRIs
(B) Psychostimulants
(C) Atypical antipsychotics
(D) Mood stabilizers
(E) Anxiolytics

CHAPTER 13

Research

Research Methods

475. Which type of investigation is typically used to explore efficacy of one psychological intervention versus another and includes placement of participants in different groups?

(A) Single subject study
(B) Randomized controlled trial
(C) Semistructured interview
(D) Ethnography
(E) Meta-analysis

476. Which is the best way to operationalize levels of depression in a study on depression?

(A) Scores on the Beck Depression Index
(B) Presence of at least one symptom of depression
(C) Meeting diagnostic criteria for depression
(D) Number of times an individual cries
(E) Asking a yes or no question about depression

477. A sample of research participants is typically drawn from

(A) cases
(B) individual subjects
(C) world representation
(D) a population
(E) a subsample

478. Connie designed an experiment to explore if play therapy for children with siblings with disabilities impacts students' school performance. What is the independent variable?

   (A) Play therapy
   (B) Children with siblings with disabilities
   (C) School performance
   (D) Performance in play therapy
   (E) Siblings' school performance

479. If a psychological test is repeatedly administered to a group of people with the same or very similar results, this test shows

   (A) consistency
   (B) reliability
   (C) validity
   (D) significance
   (E) variability

480. Which is a limitation of survey methods for psychological research?

   (A) Reliance on self-report data
   (B) Access to large samples
   (C) Information about nonobservable behaviors
   (D) Relatively low cost
   (E) None of the above

481. Study results showed that the greater amount of physical exercise an individual gets is associated with higher scores on a quality of life scale. How are these two variables related?

   (A) There is a large variance.
   (B) There is a small variance.
   (C) The variables are negatively correlated.
   (D) The variables are positively correlated.
   (E) There is no correlation between the variables.

482. A researcher who watches social behavior of children at a town pool in order to explore perceived temperament and social interactions is using which research method?

   (A) Case study
   (B) Naturalistic observation
   (C) Experimental design
   (D) Laboratory observation
   (E) Test

483. In a psychological experiment, the response that an individual has to a certain treatment is called the

(A) sample
(B) independent variable
(C) dependent variable
(D) hypothesis
(E) experimental group

484. When the entire population has an equal chance of being chosen for a study, this is called

(A) sampling
(B) random sampling
(C) random assignment
(D) population sampling
(E) population assignment

485. Adrian wants to know if participation in psychoeducation groups impacts amount of alcohol use by college students at large state colleges. If he designs a study to explore the subject, what is the independent variable?

(A) Alcohol use by college students
(B) Psychoeducation group
(C) Design of the psychoeducation group
(D) Large state colleges
(E) Alcohol-use levels before formation of group

486. A child development assessment that measures only language skills but not motor skills lacks which important aspect of measurements?

(A) Reliability
(B) Test-retest
(C) Consistency
(D) Bias
(E) Validity

487. A double-blind experiment can help limit which type of research bias?

(A) Sampling bias
(B) Subject bias
(C) Measurement bias
(D) Experimenter bias
(E) None of the above

488. Which of the following is NOT a purpose of psychological research?
  (A) To further understand behaviors
  (B) To inform the practice of psychology
  (C) To describe all aspects of psychological phenomena
  (D) To better predict outcomes
  (E) To measure different psychological phenomena

489. The population of a town in Texas includes 1,000 adults more than 50 years old. The names of these adults are on an alphabetical list. The researchers choose every fourth name to call and include in a study on mental health and aging. What type of sampling are the researchers doing?
  (A) Snowball sampling
  (B) Convenience sampling
  (C) Random sampling
  (D) Systematic sampling
  (E) Accidental sampling

490. Which type of research methodology helps to establish cause-and-effect relationships?
  (A) Experimental design
  (B) Naturalistic design
  (C) Survey design
  (D) Case study
  (E) Laboratory observation

Research Ethics

491. Researchers must get _____ from research participants who choose to continue in a study after reviewing procedures and possible risks associated with participation.
  (A) A debriefing
  (B) Permission
  (C) Informed consent
  (D) Approval
  (E) Confidentiality

492. Which strategy is NOT an ethical research practice?
- (A) Reviewing study purposes
- (B) Explaining participant rights
- (C) Reviewing expectations of study
- (D) Having participants agree to stay in the study for the entire duration
- (E) Debriefing participants after the study

493. What research technique is used to conceal the purpose of the study, often leading to ethical questions?
- (A) Deception
- (B) Informed consent
- (C) Double-blind
- (D) Placebo
- (E) Trickery

494. Dr. Plumb must present her research for review for ethical methodology to which group that evaluates human subjects research at her university?
- (A) Dissertation committee
- (B) Provost office
- (C) Institutional review board
- (D) Ethics committee
- (E) Ombudsman

495. Which ethically guided procedure makes potential subjects aware of their participation in psychological research, the expectations, and the potential risks?
- (A) Approval
- (B) Informed consent
- (C) Anonymity
- (D) Confidentiality
- (E) None of the above

496. During the Stanford Prison Experiment, participants acted in ways that damaged others' in the study. Which ethical principle did this research violate?
- (A) Informed consent
- (B) Confidentiality
- (C) Do no harm
- (D) Anonymity
- (E) Approval

497. Which research technique is sometimes used to limit participant bias?

(A) Informed consent
(B) Case study
(C) Survey design
(D) Deception
(E) None of the above

498. Which ethical principle involves keeping identifying information about participants private?

(A) Informed consent
(B) Institutional review board approval
(C) Do no harm
(D) Confidentiality
(E) None of the above

499. Which step do researchers sometimes take at the end of a subject's participation in research to further explain the study purposes and why certain things were done, let the subject talk about his or her experience, and provide resources for ongoing support?

(A) Group meeting
(B) Psychotherapy session
(C) Debriefing
(D) Deception
(E) Informed consent

500. In Milgram's famous experiment, participants believed they were involved in a study on learning when they were actually in a study on obedience. Which research approach was being used?

(A) Confidentiality
(B) Deception
(C) Informed consent
(D) Anonymity
(E) Debriefing

ANSWERS

Chapter 1: Biological Basis of Behavior

1. (B) Nucleus size is not a factor in gene expression. Gene expression is impacted by numerous factors. The environment outside of the cell, including an organism's behaviors (A) and temperature (D), as well as the timing of reproduction (C) alter the biochemistry inside the cell.

2. (D) A phenotype is what is observed in the organism, including traits, behaviors, and characteristics. *Gene transmission* (A) is a general term regarding traits that are passed on through the hereditary process. Choice (B) is the definition for a *dominant gene*. Choice (C) is the definition for *genotype*.

3. (B) The number of cells in the typical human cell is 46. Sex cells, including the ovaries in females and the sperm in males, contain only 23 cells (C).

4. (C) A recessive allele must be paired with another recessive allele on the corresponding gene in order for that trait to be expressed. For example, two recessive alleles for blue eyes exist and correspond in order for blue eyes to be the phenotype.

5. (E) Polygenetic inheritance involves inheriting traits for certain qualities from many genes rather than just one gene. Some mental disorders are thought to be transmitted through polygenetic inheritance.

6. (D) Twin studies are often used to explore the impact of genetics and also the impact of genetics versus the environment. The population of identical twins is not large, and finding identical twins who fit research criteria and want to participate is sometimes quite challenging.

7. (B) Heritability is a mathematical estimate that is used to explore the extent to which genetic and environmental factors influence differences in individuals. For example, the level of intelligence may be measured in a certain population to explore the genetic and environmental influences.

8. (E) Genes, family environment, prenatal environment, and peer relationships influence psychological traits. Other factors, including culture, also are known to influence psychological traits. There are very few factors that are internal or external to the individual that are not thought to influence psychological traits.

9. (D) The degree to which trait differences between individuals in a population can be attributed to genes can be gleaned through heritability estimates. The other choices are not found through heritability estimates. The use and generalizability of heritability estimates must be closely considered.

10. (B) Natural selection, a concept originated by Charles Darwin, describes the concept of certain traits being reproduced more frequently than others based on the advantage of these traits for survival of the species. Natural selection is a building block for the concept of evolution (C).

11. (B) A mutation is an error that occurs when DNA is copied, or is a rearrangement of DNA patterns. Mutation can result in genetic disorders but also can be an aid in evolution.

12. (D) Motor neurons transmit information from the brain to the muscles and glands. Sensory neurons (B), also called afferent neurons (E), transmit information from sensory systems in the brain. Choice (A) can be eliminated as atypical is not a type of neuron.

13. (B) An axon transmits information to other parts of the body. The nucleus (A) does not transmit data out, and the dendrite (C) is responsible for carrying information from the body to the neuron. The myelin sheath (D) wraps around axons to provide protection and other functions. The cell body (E) contains the nucleus.

14. (E) Although glial cells do provide a protective covering for axons, they are not involved in temperature regulation. Glial cells carry out many critical functions in addition to those listed in the other choices.

15. (B) Serotonin, norepinephrine, and dopamine are examples of neurotransmitters. Glutamate (C) is another type of neurotransmitter. Antagonists (D) are medications that impact neurotransmitters. A neuron (A) is a type of cell, and a dendrite (E) is part of a neuron.

16. (B) Messages from neurotransmitters cross the synaptic cleft to reach other neurons. A receptor site is the site of a neuron that is receiving messages from the neurotransmitter. The adrenal cortex (D) is part of the endocrine system, not the nervous system. The cerebral cortex (C) is the outer layer of the brain, not the space between neurons. The hypothalamus (E) helps provide a linking function between the nervous system and the endocrine system.

17. (D) SSRIs block the reuptake of serotonin, leaving increased amounts of serotonin in the synaptic cleft. Different classes of medications do serve other functions with regard to neurotransmitters, but these functions typically target other neurotransmitters.

18. (D) The parasympathetic nervous system restores the body to its typical resting state after arousal. The sympathetic nervous system (C) is responsible for mobilizing the body under stress or arousal. The parasympathetic nervous system is part of the peripheral nervous system, not the central nervous system (A). The central nervous system includes the spinal cord (E) and the brain. The somatic nervous system (B) is part of the peripheral nervous system but not part of the autonomic nervous system like the parasympathetic nervous system.

19. (A) The somatic nervous system carries motor and sensory information to and from the central nervous system. Choice (B) describes the somatic nervous system as only receiving messages, and incorrectly names the system with which the somatic system communicates. Choice (C) describes the main function of the central nervous system. Choices (D) and (E) describe the functions of the sympathetic and parasympathetic nervous systems.

20. (C) The sympathetic nervous system is responsible for arousing a response in a time of stress. Choices (A), (B), and (D) are other parts of the peripheral nervous system with other responsibilities. The brain (E) is a key part of the central nervous system.

21. (A) The left brain is responsible for verbal skills while the right brain is associated with creative thinking. The left brain is associated with both logic and objective thinking (C and D).

22. (C) The endocrine system is a system of glands that produce hormones. The glands and hormones of the endocrine system do impact the other systems of the body. For example, the reproductive systems (D) of both males and females contain hormones. Some hormones are gender specific.

23. (B) The thyroid gland can become overactive (hyperthyroidism) or underactive (hypothyroidism), leading to changes in mood. The pineal gland (A) is associated with light exposure and activity levels. The pituitary gland (C) is responsible for regulating the other glands of the endocrine system. A male sex gland is called testes (D). The adrenal glands (E) are mainly responsible for releasing stress-related hormones.

24. (D) Transcranial magnetic stimulation is a procedure used to treat some psychological disorders, but it is not used to study or view the brain. Transcranial magnetic stimulation is not an instrument; it is a procedure. All of the other choices are different methods of looking at the brain.

25. (C) The adrenal glands are mainly responsible for releasing stress-related hormones. Choice (A) describes the functions of the testes and ovum. Choice (D) describes the function of the thyroid, and the thyroid functioning can impact mood (B). The pineal gland is mainly involved in rest-related functions (E).

26. (B) The pons is responsible for producing chemicals related to the sleep and wake cycle. The pons also serves other functions in the brain, including motor control and attention. The medulla (A) and the midbrain (E) are other parts of the brain stem. The thalamus (D) sits on top of the midbrain, and it passes sensory and motor information to other parts of the brain.

27. (A) The frontal lobe is involved in regulating emotions and behaviors, and damage to the frontal lobe can lead to mood and personality changes. The cerebellum (E) is not a lobe of the brain. The other lobes (B, C, and D) serve other functions in the brain and body.

28. (B) Because the temporal lobe is responsible for regulating the sense of smell, an injury to the temporal lobe could cause a loss of the sense of smell. The frontal lobe (A) is not involved in sensory activities. The parietal lobe (C) links sensory functions to other parts of the body. The occipital lobe (D) is involved in the sense of sight and processing sight-related information. Finally, the cerebellum (E) controls balance, among other things.

29. (C) Nonverbal tasks are a function of the right brain. The other choices listed are functions of the left brain. The different functioning of each side of the brain is often referred to as lateralization. Although each side of the brain is responsible for different tasks, the sides do function closely together.

30. (B) The amygdala is involved in evaluating emotional responses. It also stores implicit memories related to these responses. The hippocampus (A) is also involved in storing memories. The corpus callosum (D) and the spinal cord (E) serve important brain functions but are not part of the limbic system. The hypothalamus (C) is responsible for helping the body maintain homeostasis, including regulating sleep and eating cycles.

31. (B) Neuroplasticity refers to the change in neuron patterns and connections throughout one's development through the life cycle. Lateralization (C) refers to the different functions of the two sides of the brain. The other choices are words that could be used in reference to neuroplasticity but are more general vocabulary terms that do not specifically refer to this process in the brain.

32. (D) The parietal lobe is involved in sensory functioning and motor functioning. The other choices are different lobes of the brain that are involved in other processes.

33. (C) Afferent neurons, also called sensory neurons, are responsible for bringing sensory information to the brain. Interneurons (B) assist neurons in communicating with each other. Motor neurons (A) transmit information from the brain to the muscles and glands.

34. (C) Endorphins are associated with inhibiting pain in moments of pain, extreme danger, or other circumstances. Serotonin (A), epinephrine (B), and dopamine (D) are generally associated with emotional functioning. Acetylcholine (E) is associated with arousal and attention.

35. (C) The occipital lobe is associated with processing visual information. Information gathered by the structures of the eye is transformed into meaning with the help of the occipital lobe.

36. (B) Oxytocin is associated with labor and with lactation. Pair bonding and orgasm are also associated with oxytocin, leading to the nickname for oxytocin as the love hormone.

37. (D) Humans have two adrenal glands, and they are associated with responses to stress. Cortisol and adrenaline are key hormones that are regulated by the adrenal glands.

38. (A) The action potential of a neuron is critical in neuron-to-neuron communication. Action potential occurs when the neuron is depolarized and facilitates ions traveling across the cell membranes.

39. (C) An antagonist blocks the action of neurotransmitters. For example, the presence of an antagonist may prevent neurotransmitters from binding to receptors.

40. (B) The somatic nervous system is associated with voluntary actions, like a purposeful effort to take a step. The autonomic nervous system is associated with involuntary actions, including breathing.

41. (A) The forebrain is the largest section and contains the cerebellum, the limbic system, and many other neural networks. When we think of the brain, we are often thinking of the forebrain. The midbrain (B) and the hindbrain (C) do play important functions in the brain and the body.

42. (B) Lateralization refers to the concept that each side of the brain is responsible for different functions. Additionally, the right side of the brain is known to control left-side body functions, and the left side of the brain is associated with right-side body functions.

Chapter 2: Sensation and Perception

43. (B) The absolute threshold describes the smallest amount of a substance needed to be detected. Choice (C) is an attempt at the absolute threshold of salt but is incorrect. The difference threshold (A) describes the smallest amount of change needed for detection of the change. Choice (D) can be eliminated as it is not a term used in the sensory arena. *Sensory threshold* (E) is a broader term that encompasses both (A) and (B).

44. (A) The two notches describe the difference threshold, as Caryn could not hear the music after a one-notch change, but she could hear the music after a two-notch change. The absolute threshold (B) describes the amount, or in this case volume, of music needed to hear anything. *Sensory threshold* (D) is a term that includes both difference and absolute thresholds. Choices (C) and (E) are not sensory-related terms.

45. (B) Weber's law allows for comparison of sense sensitivities despite the different units of measurement. Fechner's law (A) is another law of sensation but does not compare sensations; it describes the strength of the sensation as being proportional to the logarithm of the stimulus intensity. Frequency theory (C) relates to the sense of sound. Choices (D) and (E) describe other concepts involving sensation and perception.

46. (C) Pressure, temperature, and pain are considered skin senses. The skin is the largest organ of the body and contains nerve endings that sense pressure, temperature, and pain. Skin senses are related to the sense of touch (D), but "touch senses" is not proper terminology. The other choices (A, B, and E) refer to other senses.

47. (B) Olfaction is another way to refer to the sense of smell. Glomeruli (A) are substances involved in the initial processing of scents. An odorant (C) is a substance with a smell. Anosmia (D) refers to a condition when someone has lost his or her sense of smell. Pheromones (E) are naturally occurring odorants that send signals to other organisms.

48. (E) Umami is the taste of savory and is associated with foods such as some meats, cheeses, and vegetables. The word is of Japanese origin. The other choices, sweet (A), salty (B), bitter (C), and sour (D), may at times be associated with the foods mentioned, but they are not mainly associated with these foods. Additionally, the description of *savory* does not fit the other choices.

49. (B) Taste buds are located in the papillae on the tongue. Receptor cells (A) are located on the taste buds and respond when they come in contact with tastants (D). Saliva (E) helps to dissolve tastants. Molecules (C) can be eliminated, as it is a general term.

50. (A) Sound waves are created by molecule movement in the environment (sometimes playing an instrument) that travels to the outer ear. The other choices are also related to sound but are not described in the question.

51. (B) A hertz is the unit of measurement that describes the frequency of sound waves in cycles per second. Decibels (D) are the units of measure that describe loudness. Octaves (A) describe pitch. Choices (C) and (E) are related to sound but are not the unit of measurement that describe the frequency of sound waves.

52. (C) Timbre describes sound quality and allows humans to differentiate different voices, different instruments even if they are playing the same note, and other specifications related to quality of sound. Frequency (A) and amplitude (B) are the two qualities of sound waves that create different sounds. Pitch (D) is created by the number of sound peaks per second, and octaves (E) are intervals between pitches.

53. (B) The location on the basilar membrane where the messages are the strongest describes place theory. Choice (A) is a partial description of frequency theory. The other choices are incorrect descriptions of place theory.

54. (B) The hammer, anvil, and stirrup are small bones in the middle ear that vibrate and send vibrations to the cochlea. These parts are unique to the ear and are not involved in the other senses.

55. (C) The visible spectrum goes from violet (at 400 nanometers) to red (at 700 nanometers) and the rainbow of colors in between. Nanometer (D) is the unit of measure used when describing light waves. Choices (A) and (B) are not terms related to light or sight. The trichromatic theory (E) is related to sight but is not described in this question.

56. (B) Rods are photoreceptors that respond to varying levels of light. Cones (A) assist in recognizing color sensations. Pupils (C), iris (D), and fovea (E) are parts of the eye but are not responsible for responding to light levels.

57. (B) Retinal messages pass through the bipolar cells to the ganglion. The axons of the ganglion come together to form an optic nerve that carries messages to the brain. Choices (A) and (D) do not include the ganglion. Choice (C) does not include the bipolar cells and incorrectly designates functions for other parts of the eye. Choice (E) does not include bipolar cells or the optic nerve.

58. (D) The axons of the ganglion cells form the optic nerve. This is a key structure in passing visual information to the brain in order to enable sight.

59. (D) The fovea is responsible for the acuity of vision. The connection between cones and bipolar cells in the fovea assists in this process. The fovea is a part of the retina (C). The optic nerve (E) passes visual information to the brain. The iris (A) allows light to pass into the eye, and the cornea (B) regulates the amount of light that contacts the retina.

60. (A) Saturation determines the vividness of hues. The more gray a color has in it, the less saturation that color has. Colors are considered chromatic (D) or achromatic (C), and human vision is based on three colors, making it trichromatic (E). Brightness (B) is associated with the amount of white a color has in it.

61. (C) Brightness allows for differentiation between black and gray (as well as white) and is present in colors that have hues as well. Black and gray are achromatic (D) because they do not have a hue (B). Saturation (A) describes a hue, and chromatic colors (E) are colors that have a hue.

62. (D) Red, blue, and green are the colors associated with the trichromatic theory of color. Trichromatic theory states that these three colors provide the base for the large spectrum of colors we see. Colors such as yellow and purple contain elements of the base colors of red, blue, and green; therefore, choices (A), (B), and (E) are incorrect. White, black, and gray (C) are achromatic colors.

63. (B) This description is of the opponent-process theory. Huvich and Jameson (C) developed the theory, but it is not named for them. The other major theory of color, trichromatic color theory (A), does not pair colors together, rather it pairs color hues with different types of cones; it was developed by Young and further refined by Helmholtz (E). Color-blindness (D) is a different concept altogether.

64. (A) The red circle is an afterimage and is thought to go from green to red because of the opponent-process theory. The receptors that initially saw green go through an adaptation process after looking at green for that period of time.

65. (C) Evan's condition is known as monochromatic color-blindness because he sees only pairs on the opponent-process spectrum. People with dichromatic color-blindness (B) have difficulty with the red-green spectrum but see other colors. Choice (D) is a type of dichromatic color-blindness. Many cases of color-blindness are due to genetics, but genetic color-blindness (E) is not a specific condition. Trichromatic color-blindness (A) refers to sensitivity of the eye to one of the three core pigments. In this case, Evan does not see any of the pigments.

66. (C) Sensation is the sensory experience and is a passive process. Perception is the patterning, interpretation, and meaning making of the experience. Choice (E) is not correct, as it describes sensation as an active rather than passive process. The other choices also incorrectly describe either sensation or perception.

67. (D) Closure refers to humans' tendency to see items as complete shapes or figures even when parts are missing. In other words, we perceive the closure of the shape or figure when it may not be present. Contours (E) are a part of our perception that assist in closing figures or completing figures. The other choices are other principles of perception but not the one described in the question.

68. (B) Proximity states that humans tend to perceive things grouped together in groups rather than separately. Choices (A), (C), and (D) are different principles of perception. Contours (E) are part of perception but are not related to proximity or groups of items.

69. (B) The concept of figure and ground allows us to distinguish between items. At times this includes items in the foreground and the background of a photo as the question describes. Figure and ground is part of our perceptual organization (C). Distinction (D) and constancy (E) are other principles of perception. Continuation (A) is a different principle of perception.

70. (B) Perceptual constancy allows us to see some things as not changing despite sensory evidence that is changing. Our previous environmental information informs the perception of white snow even in varying environments.

71. (C) Linear perspective is the concept that explains why parallel lines appear to converge as they get farther away from the viewer. This can be seen on floors that have lines across them and even on drawings that show depth. The other choices describe different concepts related to monocular cues.

72. (B) Pictorial cues create the sense of three dimensions on a flat surface. Artists frequently use techniques around pictorial cues to show dimensions and depth in their work. The other choices are other types of monocular cues but do not specifically describe dimensions on a flat surface.

73. (B) Binocular disparity is the concept that each eye sees things from a slightly different angle. The brain uses messages from each eye to create depth perception. The example of the three-dimensional glasses and movie uses binocular disparity, as the different lens glasses make for different messages going to each eye. This causes binocular disparity and gives the movie "depth" that it did not have without the audience wearing the glasses.

74. (B) Apparent movement is a perception of motion of still objects. The perception comes from presenting appropriately timed intervals of stimuli. In this case, flipping quickly through the flip-book would show the apparent movement but flipping slowly through the book would not have the same effect. The other choices are related to perception but not as described in this question.

75. (B) The concept of figure and ground allows people to separate background and the object. This concept aids in perception and allows us to see figures on a page.

76. (C) An illusion is a misinterpretation of information. It leads to an error in perception. There are many different artistic examples of illusions where the perception of depth or of movement is present although depth and movement are not actually happening.

77. (C) Continuity allows us to perceive a series of dots in a certain pattern as a continuous figure.

78. (E) Gestalt theory looks at the whole and sees the whole as greater than its individual parts. Regarding perception, looking at a group of lines as a group, rather than as each individual line, aids in perception.

79. (D) The concept of figure and ground is at play when looking at this type of figure. This is called a reversible figure. The lamp can be the figure and the face can also be the figure in this case.

80. (C) Perceptual constancy allows Tyler to view the church as one size although it changes size in the visual data. Tyler does not perceive the church as growing as he moves closer toward it.

Chapter 3: Consciousness

81. (E) REM sleep mirrors wakefulness, with brain activity, respiration, and heart rate mirroring wakefulness, although an individual in REM is sound asleep and difficult to wake. Stage 1 (A) begins the sleep cycle. Stages 2 and 3 (B and C) are characterized by the slowing down of heart rate and respiration. Stage 4 (D) is very deep sleep.

82. (A) The question describes some characteristics of stage 1 sleep. Stage 1 sleep is also characterized by alpha waves and a slowing pulse. One marked difference between stage 1 and the other sleep stages is the ability of someone to wake from that stage. The other sleep stages are much more difficult for people to wake from.

83. (C) There are many different theories about dreaming, but there is not one concrete proven answer for why humans dream. Therefore, choice (C) is the most accurate answer. Each answer in (A), (B), and (D) describes one of the theories behind dreaming. Although dreaming is an individual process, the reason behind dreaming does not vary from person to person; therefore, choice (E) is not accurate.

84. (D) Insomnia refers to a difficulty falling asleep or staying asleep, and it results in the individual getting a great deal less sleep than is needed. The other choices are different types of sleep disorders but are not described in Karen's case.

85. (D) The question describes the main characteristics of narcolepsy. Those who suffer from narcolepsy can also have bouts of insomnia (C). Narcolepsy is considered a dysomnia, related to amount, quality, and timing of sleep rather than a parasomnia (E), which relates to behaviors and physiological events during sleep.

86. (B) A look at sleep patterns through the life cycle shows decreased sleep progressing from children into older adulthood. Babies need and typically get the most amount of sleep. Older adults spend a great deal of sleep time in awake states according to previous sleep studies.

87. (B) Sleep apnea is characterized by difficulty breathing during sleep. Those who suffer from sleep apnea may wake up coughing or grasping for breath, interrupting their sleep.

88. (D) Stage 4 of sleep is associated with slow delta waves. Stage 4 sleep is the deepest level of sleep and is often associated with dreaming. The other stages of sleep are associated with different types of brain waves.

89. (C) The sleep stages progress from stage 4, to stage 3, to stage 2, and then to stage 1, after which the sleeper progresses to REM sleep. This is a typical sleep cycle.

90. (C) The latent content of a dream is the underlying meaning. The manifest and latent contents of dreams are Freudian theories. Dream interpretation is an ongoing technique in some areas of psychology.

91. (D) REM sleep mirrors wakefulness; therefore, it is also called paradoxical sleep. A paradox in any situation contradicts common sense. Because REM sleep looks like wakefulness on EEGs and in physiological responses, it is thought to be paradoxical.

92. (C) Circadian rhythms are natural 24-hour cycles in humans. These rhythms are disrupted when traveling across times zones, and they are especially difficult to adjust to when traveling west to east. Circadian rhythms are commonly called the body clock.

93. (A) Increased accidents and a compromised immune system are associated with sleep deprivation. Sleep deprivation is also associated with obesity, not weight loss as indicated by (B) and (D). Mood disorders (D) and workplace absenteeism (B) are also associated with sleep deprivation. Many other psychological and physiological side effects are associated with sleep deprivation.

94. (E) Individuals are often instructed to get out of bed if sleep has not come in a reasonable amount of time. This strategy allows someone to then restart the process around getting ready for bed and sleep. Limiting caffeine intake, ensuring darkness in the bedroom, and using the bedroom for only sleep-related activities can be useful for individuals with sleep difficulties.

95. (D) Stage 4, considered very deep sleep, is the stage in which people are most likely to sleepwalk. Sometimes children sleepwalk and eventually grow out of this habit. There are cases in which sleepwalking behaviors are quite dangerous.

96. (D) Alertness implies awareness and clear consciousness rather than an altered state of consciousness. The other choices are different types of altered states of consciousness.

97. (B) Awareness of our experience, environment, thoughts, and feelings while awake is referred to as our consciousness. Alertness (A) is a part of consciousness but not the entire picture. Introspection (D) is a way individuals become aware of their own consciousness; sometimes people achieve this through a practice called mindfulness (C). Unconsciousness (E) is the opposite of the conscious awareness described in the question.

98. (C) The cognitive unconscious is outside of our awareness but plays a large part in helping us to organize and perceive the world. We are unable to use introspection (A) to describe the cognitive unconscious, as introspection is a conscious process. Dreaming (B) is one of the alternative states of consciousness.

99. (A) Hypnosis is known to act as an analgesic, or pain reliever, for some medical conditions. Although individuals may be open to more suggestions under hypnosis, it does not eliminate free will (D). Hypnosis is not known to produce changes in depressed mood (B) or in memory (E). There are many myths about what happens to people under hypnosis, including the myth that people have increased physical strength under hypnosis (C).

100. (C) This is the dissociation theory of hypnosis and describes the altered state of consciousness that is produced during hypnosis. The social influence (B) and social cognitive (E) theories of hypnosis refer to the suggestibility (A) that can occur in a hypnotic state. Chanting (D) is associated with meditation.

101. (B) Meditation mirrors the state of relaxed wakefulness. Hypnosis (C) and meditation are similar states of consciousness, but meditation does not have the same suggestive qualities sometimes associated with hypnosis. Meditation does not mirror sleeping brain activity (A and D) or depressant altered consciousness (E), despite its impact on slowing heart and respiratory rates.

102. (D) The question describes a meditation practice that Larry is engaged in. All of the other choices are known effects of meditation.

103. (A) Alcohol consumption is associated with decreased inhibition overall. This causes people to make decisions they may not have made had they not been drinking. The other answer choices describe possible consequences of drinking but the descriptor (*increased; decreased*) is incorrect.

104. (B) Methylphenidate (Ritalin), dextroamphetamine, and amphetamine (Adderall) are stimulants that are prescription drugs used to treat ADHD. In general, stimulants have both legitimate and illegitimate uses. Stimulants increase the level of arousal in the body.

105. (D) Although alcohol consumption sometimes occurs during mealtimes, food preferences and alcohol use are not related. The other answers are all factors associated with alcohol use.

106. (D) *Dependence* is sometimes used as a synonym of *addiction*. Dependence is associated with physical addiction, including withdrawal symptoms. Opiate use (A), abuse (B), and intoxication (C) describe precursors to dependence. Opiate tolerance (E) occurs over periods of use and is a symptom of dependence.

107. (B) Drug tolerance refers to the need for increased amounts of a drug to produce the same effect. Therefore, the results of the same amount of the drug are reduced over time. Drug tolerance occurs with frequent use of a drug, and different individuals experience this phenomenon at different rates.

108. (C) Hallucinogens can cause users to hallucinate, thus producing perceptions that may not in fact be present. Users of hallucinogens describe seeing and hearing things that were not present. Hallucinations are also a symptom of some psychiatric disorders, including schizophrenia. Ongoing psychosis is a dangerous side effect of hallucinogens.

109. (E) Cocaine is a stimulant, and stimulants have an effect opposite of "calmness" on their users. The other choices describe effects of cocaine, as well as some other stimulants. Additional side effects include sleeplessness and irritability.

110. (D) An SSRI does not contribute to drug addiction. There are some prescription medications that are considered narcotics and do have addictive qualities, but SSRIs are not among these. The other choices are known to have an influence on drug dependence.

Chapter 4: Learning and Memory

111. (C) An unconditioned response is one that the organism brings into the situation. It is not learned in the learning process (classical conditioning). A conditioned stimulus (A) is a condition introduced in the process of learning. A conditioned response (B) is a response to learning. Habituation (D) is a decline in response to a situation once it becomes familiar; it is a product of learning. Learned helplessness (E) is also a product of learning and can result in continuing to access negative stimuli with the same negative results.

112. (B) The conditioned stimulus, the bell in Pavlov's experiment, is a previously neutral stimulus that is conditioned to elicit a response that it did not previously elicit. The bell elicited no response when the dogs first heard it, but when paired with meat powder repeatedly, it began to elicit salivation.

113. (A) The chemical is the US (unconditioned stimulus) because it causes the squirrels to get sick. Mr. Goodman's trees are originally neutral stimuli, but when paired with the chemical, they become the conditioned stimuli (CS). The conditioned response, which is frequently the desired response in classical conditioning, is the squirrels avoiding the trees.

114. (A) For Jason, the plane is a stimulus that was previously neutral and now elicits a conditioned response (B) of nausea.

115. (B) The unconditioned stimulus produces a response automatically and without prior exposure or training. The response is sometimes psychological and sometimes physical in nature. In the case of Little Albert, the unconditioned stimulus is the loud noise.

116. (B) The description of Margo and her symptoms lead to the possibility that she has developed a phobia. Some of the characteristics of phobia are present in her symptoms. Additionally, the question describes a classical conditioning scenario where the unconditioned stimulus (bullying) causes the unconditioned response (crying, sadness). The conditioned stimulus (the pool) was paired with the unconditioned response; therefore, pools began to elicit conditioned responses for Margo.

117. (C) This answer describes spontaneous recovery. In spontaneous recovery, the learned response can come back if the presentation of the conditioned stimulus without the unconditioned stimulus is not repeatedly reinforced. Although spontaneous recovery can occur, the conditioned response is typically weaker than the response created before extinction.

118. (C) Systematic desensitization is a treatment based on classical conditioning theory. It involves making a hierarchy of fears and moving up the hierarchy to eventually address the phobia and relieve the person experiencing it. Systematic desensitization involves relaxation techniques, some of which come out of meditation practices (E), but the answer does not describe meditation. Flooding (D) involves the opposite approach of exposing the individual to the fearful stimuli in a rapid way. Psychopharmacology (A) and cognitive behavioral therapy (B) are other interventions sometimes used for phobias but are not described in the question.

119. (B) Because Kerri now avoids eating shrimp, she experiences what is called a taste aversion. In terms of classical conditioning, the previously neutral stimuli (CS), shrimp, is paired with an unconditioned stimulus (US), queasiness. This now produces a conditioned response (CR), avoiding shrimp. It was the presence of the queasiness during that one incident that produced this response for Kerri.

120. (A) This answer describes extinction. In the Pavlov's dogs example, if the bell were repeatedly rung without the presentation of the meat powder, the dogs would eventually stop salivating from the bell being rung.

121. (B) Phobias are associated with classical conditioning. The case of Little Albert showed a young infant developing a phobia-like reaction to a stimuli that he originally responded positively to. But when it was paired with a loud noise, he had a different reaction. Classical conditioning is one way phobias may develop. The other choices are other psychological conditions but are not thought to be associated with classical conditioning.

122. (D) The conditioned stimulus is paired with the unconditioned stimulus, and these factors together produce the unconditioned response. Then, with the removal of the unconditioned stimulus, the conditioned stimulus continues to produce the conditioned response. The other responses do not have the conditioned response, unconditioned stimulus, and conditioned stimulus in the proper order.

123. (B) Operant conditioning is learning that occurs based on being paired with rewards or punishments. Classical conditioning (A) describes learning in which a naturally occurring response is elicited by a formerly neutral stimulus. Higher-order conditioning (D) is a concept within classical conditioning. A reinforcer (E) occurs after a behavior, and it increases the likelihood of the behavior occurring again. Learning that is outside the conscious awareness of the individual and does not result in an immediate behavioral response is called latent learning (C).

124. (B) Because the dog treat is added to the dog's experience and it is intended to increase the likelihood of the behavior of sitting, the dog treat is a positive reinforcer. A negative reinforcer (A) is something that is removed to increase the likelihood of the behavior. A partial reinforcer (C) is intended to reinforce only some of the organism's responses. Both negative and positive punishments (D and E) are intended to decrease the likelihood of the behavior.

125. (E) The consequence is something that is taken away in order to influence the behavior to go away, making it a negative punishment. The word *negative* refers to the fact that something is taken away. Positive punishment (D) is something added. If Thomas were made to clean the bathrooms after talking back, that would represent a positive punishment. Reinforcers (A, B, and C) are used to increase, not eliminate, behaviors.

126. (D) Effective punishment does not include steadily increasing the punishment. In fact, consistency is very important in this type of learning. In addition, punishment needs to occur right after the behavior (C), so steadily increasing the punishment would not associate it as closely to the behavior. The other choices (A, B, and E) are conditions needed for punishment.

127. (A) Shaping involves rewarding behaviors that are similar to the ultimate desired response in order to eventually elicit the desired response. Fixed-ratio reinforcement (B) and interval reinforcement (C) are different types of patterned reinforcements. Latent learning (D) does not result in an immediate behavioral response. Rewards are not involved in classical conditioning (E).

128. (A) The question describes negative reinforcement because a stimulus is taken away in the effort to increase a particular behavior. Positive reinforcement (B) involves adding a stimulus rather than taking one away. Variable-ratio reinforcement (E) involves scheduled reinforcement. Both negative and positive punishments (C and D) are used to decrease the frequencies of behaviors.

129. (B) Danna's decision to not study because she believes studying has no impact on her scores is learned helplessness. Learned helplessness involves an acquired sense of a lack of control or mastery over certain conditions, and it inhibits learning. The other choices describe other learning conditions, not conditions that inhibit learning.

130. (B) Because there are a fixed number of responses that Phillip needs before his reward, this is considered a fixed-ratio schedule. In variable-ratio schedules (A), the number of responses needed for reward changes. In interval schedules (E), reward occurs after a certain interval of time. Partial and negative reinforcements (C and D) are types of reinforcement but not types of reinforcement schedules.

131. (A) Ryan has had the benefit of vicarious learning because he has witnessed his brother's behavior and learned from this example about how not to behave. Shaping (B) is a staged approach to learning, and this question does not describe different stages. Latent learning (C), cognitive learning (D), and prepared learning (E) do not occur on a conscious level.

132. (C) Jamal has created a cognitive map that is stored as a mental image. Mirror neurons (A) aid in learning but are not described in the question. Vicarious learning (B) occurs by witnessing others and is a type of social learning (E). Insight (D) describes a learning moment whereby an individual gains a clear understanding of something, sometimes by making an association.

133. (D) Despite the vast differences in biological makeup and communication, humans and nonhumans learn in many of the same ways, including operant conditioning, classical conditioning, and latent learning. Many learning experiments have been done on human and nonhuman subjects that have indicated the many learning similarities. The other choices do not accurately describe human and nonhuman learning.

134. (B) Over time the fear experienced extinction. Extinction occurs when the condition is presented repeatedly over time without the unconditioned stimulus. In this case, we can assume that Sabrina saw and experienced dogs over the past few years without being bitten. These are the conditions needed for extinction. Spontaneous recovery (A) occurs after extinction.

135. (B) Operant conditioning is associated with learning a new behavior through rewards and punishments. Classical conditioning (A) is associated with responses that occur naturally but are paired with other stimulus to create the conditioned response. Latent learning (C), vicarious learning (D), and cognitive learning (E) are other types of learning but would not be used to train a dog to fetch a ball.

136. (B) Latent learning is learning that occurs naturally without reinforcement. Operant conditioning (A) can include both positive and negative reinforcers (C). Shaping (D) is associated with staged reinforcement toward a goal. Extinction (E) is the process of changing a learned response.

137. (D) Carrie has experienced incidental learning. Incidental learning is not purposeful and often occurs without awareness that learning is occurring. Carrie remembers the highlights that she learned about the country and what she did there because of her experiences while on vacation.

138. (C) The three steps of the memory process are encoding, storage, and retrieval. *Acquisition* (B) is another word for *encoding*. Recall (A) is a type of retrieval and occurs when using memory to answer a question.

139. (A) Primacy and recency effect describe the phenomenon of memory that allows humans to remember the beginning and end of the list more easily than remembering the middle of a list. The other answers are not accurate.

140. (B) The primacy and recency effects show the interplay between long-term memory and short-term memory. Because of the time and ability to rehearse the beginning parts of a list, chances are increased that these words will be transferred to long-term memory, thus the primacy effect. The end parts of a list are likely still stored in short-term memory when they are recalled.

141. (C) Chunking is the process of combining a list of numbers into larger item chunks during working memory; therefore, the individual remembers numbers as chunks instead of individual numbers. This allows for more memory. Maintenance rehearsal (B) and mnemonics (E) are other tactics used for memory but are not the best tactics to memorize a large list. Deep processing (D) describes a memory strategy that involves making meaning of what is being memorized. Recall (A) is a part of the overall memory processes. The other choices are strategies to increase recall ability.

142. (D) Mnemonics are purposeful strategies for memorization and often involve making connections to other things or other linguistic strategies to aid in memory. The other choices are memory strategies but are not described in the question.

143. (C) Maintenance rehearsal, also called rote rehearsal, refers to repeating information over and over again. Because it does not involve associating the information with previously stored information, or a greater understanding of the information, it is less successful with getting information into long-term memory. Choices (A), (B), and (D) do involve strategies that can assist in information being transferred to long-term memory. Recall (E) describes the retrieval of information.

144. (B) Learning and understanding have repeatedly been shown as primary factors of getting information into long-term memory. Rote memorization without attention to meaning or understanding does not transfer to long-term memory.

145. (B) *Working memory* is another way to refer to *short-term memory*. The term indicates ideas and thoughts an individual is currently working on. Attention (C) and schemata (D) are other concepts of memory, but they are not synonyms for *short-term memory*. Present memory (A) is not a term in the memory literature although short-term memory is present based. Procedural memory (E) is a type of long-term memory.

146. (B) Laurie's visit provided her with retrieval cues that then activated her memory. She had not forgotten these experiences but had no access to them until returning to the place where the memories occurred. Implicit memories (A) cannot be expressed and the experience is outside of consciousness. The other choices are concepts in memory but are not described in the question.

147. (E) Primacy effect refers to the tendency to remember the beginning parts of a list, and recency effect refers to the tendency to remember the end parts of a list. Choices (A) and (B) only describe a part of Adrian's experience. Free recall (C) is the process of recalling items in any sort of sequence. Working memory (D) describes thoughts that are in one's current experience or that are being thought about in the moment.

148. (C) The amygdala is responsible for storing emotional memories. The frontal lobe (A) and hippocampus (D) are involved in storing semantic and episodic memories. The motor cortex (E) stores procedural memories. The prefrontal cortex (B) stores short-term memories.

149. (B) Retrograde amnesia indicates a loss of memories leading up to the incident. Memories that are closer to the incident are more likely to be lost than those that had been stored long before the incident. Choice (A) describes anterograde amnesia. The other choices do not describe a specific type of amnesia.

150. (B) Retroactive interference is one way of losing memories and involves the introduction of new memories that interfere with the stored memories. Proactive interference (C) occurs when the memories already stored interfere with the newly presented information. Decay theory (A) and forgetting curve (E) involve the passage of time leading to forgetting. Amnesia (D) refers to memory loss and is typically caused by accidents or diseases.

151. (A) Decay theory states that merely the passage of time leads to the loss of memories. A small retention interval (B) would indicate that Tyler attempted to recall the memory shortly after storing it. In this case he memorized it in high school but was recalling it during law school, indicating a long passage of time. The other answers are factors leading to memory difficulties but are not described in the question.

152. (A) Attention to what is happening in the moment is required for storing items in short-term memory, while the process of storing items in long-term memory requires a greater understanding of the concept to be memorized. Students who study for a test by only memorizing terms are more likely to forget the terms after the test than students who learn and understand the material.

153. (D) A procedural memory is one that involves motor skills and habits; riding a bike is a memorized motor skill. *Working memory* (E) is another term for *short-term memory*. Episodic memories (B) involve memories of specific times and places, and emotional memories (A) involve emotional responses to stimuli. Memories of facts and concepts are called semantic memories (C).

154. (C) Because recall is improved when it is done in the environment where the material was learned, listening to Mozart is an attempt at re-creating the study environment. The other choices do not describe the environment Valari created to study for the exam, so it is unlikely they would be helpful in recalling the information.

155. (B) Context reinstatement refers to the phenomenon that increases memory retrieval when the state of mind where the learning occurred is re-created. State of mind can be physiological, mood based, or other "state-related" contexts. Re-creating the environment where the memory occurred (A) is another way to increase memory, but it is not described in the question. The other choices do not describe ways to increase memory retrieval.

156. (E) Hypnosis is not a way to improve memory. The other choices do describe known ways to encourage the passage of information from short-term to long-term memory and the recall of information later.

157. (E) Repressed memories are believed to be created as a defense mechanism to protect people from the difficult memory of the trauma. There have been controversial cases related to the recovery of repressed memories. Regardless, this type of memory is important in the study of memory. The other choices are explicit memories and, therefore, are not outside of consciousness.

158. (C) A flashbulb memory is typically associated with a large dramatic event and can cause an emotional response. In this case, Emma's memory of the hurricane is a flashbulb memory. The other memories are not described in the question.

159. (E) An implicit memory is not consciously recalled but is revealed in an individual's behaviors and responses. The other responses are all types of explicit memories (D). Explicit memories are in the conscious awareness of an individual and are consciously activated.

160. (C) Elaborate rehearsal is associated with linking new memories to stored memories to increase the time the new memory is stored in short-term memory.

161. (E) *Working memory* is another name for *short-term memory*. Experiences that are in the working memory have not yet been transferred to long-term memory. Some experiences will never be transferred to long-term memory while others will be.

162. (D) Maintenance rehearsal, also called rote rehearsal, allows a brief memory of the information. Maintenance rehearsal that does not involve an intent to store the information or associate it with something else will not result in long-term memory.

163. (B) Schema about the world includes beliefs based on past experience. This schema influences thoughts and feelings and also the attention that individuals may pay to situations and the creation of new memories. At times schema can distort memories.

164. (D) The question describes retroactive interference. In retroactive interference, the new information interferes with previously stored information. The information from the news report interfered with Barry's original memory of the incident.

165. (E) Reconstruction is the phenomenon of memories being altered each time they are retrieved. In a long court case, a witness may be expected to retrieve the memories repeatedly over long periods of time, leading to the possibility of reconstruction errors.

166. (C) Encoding involves the way in which individuals store the information. Storage in long-term memory is more likely if there is a deep understanding of the material. Although this student studied and read, the lack of understanding may have caused an encoding error.

167. (A) A flashbulb memory is one that is very vivid, often around emotionally charged incidents. Flashbulb memories are known to "flash" in people's minds when they are recalled. Autobiographical memories (D) include people's personal histories but do not involve vivid flashing.

Chapter 5: Cognition and Language

168. (A) Language, concepts, and images are the foundations of thought. Thought allows for both problem solving and decision making.

169. (B) An analogical representation is one that resembles the image someone is trying to represent. Therefore, when picturing her childhood home, the image of what it looks like comes to mind. A symbolic representation (A) does not resemble or share qualities of the image. The other choices are concepts in cognition but are not described in the question.

170. (E) The question describes symbolic representation. Sometimes when recalling a specific concept, the concept doesn't conjure a mental image that is tangible and represents the concept. It conjures up things that are similar or related to the concept. An analogical representation (D) does share similar qualities to the item it represents and is a mental image (C). Cognitive schemas (A) and prototypes (B) are different concepts in cognition.

171. (B) A prototype is a mental model that contains the most characteristic qualities of a concept. In this case, "dog" is a very common characteristic of the concept of house pets. An image (A) and a mental representation (D) refer to what is conjured up in one's head when thinking about the concept.

172. (C) This categorization is referred to as concepts, and concepts are one of the components of thought. Prototypes (D) are a type of concept. Mental representations (A) are parts of the mind, and mental images (B) are a type of mental representation. Sensory clues (E) do exist for individuals but are not described in this process of cognition.

173. (C) Framing describes the phenomenon that the way in which a problem or information is presented has an effect on decision making. This phenomenon is supported in the research. Mental images (A), mental representations (B), and prototypes (D) are cognitive concepts but not directly related to decision making. The compensatory model (E) of decision making is a rational model in which all of the factors are presented.

174. (A) Heuristics are a frequently used problem-solving method, but their limitations must be kept in mind. The generalizations made may be just that, generalizations, and may not apply to this particular problem. Choice (B) is incorrect, as heuristics are an expedient way of solving problems rather than a drawn-out method. Choice (C) indicates a long analysis process, which is not the case when using heuristics. Subgoals (E) are a part of heuristics but do not describe a disadvantage. The personal background of individuals (D) is always a factor in someone's problem-solving methods.

175. (D) Fixedness is actually a barrier to problem solving. The other choices describe problem-solving methods. Working backward (E) is an example of a heuristic method.

176. (D) Expertise is something that can help an individual become more adept at problem solving, particularly when one develops expertise in a certain area. The other choices are barriers to problem solving.

177. (B) Availability heuristics involves using examples that come up from memory to make generalizations to inform decisions. Frequency (E) (and counting) is involved in availability heuristics but is not a decision-making strategy on its own. Representative heuristics (A) and confirmation bias (C) are other heuristic decision-making strategies. Framing (D) is the influence the way a concept is presented has on decision making.

178. (D) Algorithms are most commonly used with math problems or to solve other number-related problems. Trial and error (A) and working backward (B) are not effective problem-solving strategies for calculating possible die roll outcomes. Additionally, subgoals (C) and information retrieval (E) would not help solve this type of problem.

179. (E) Hindsight bias is the tendency to see certain events as predictable. In this question we can see the connection that Carlos made to his decision to drive in the snow, but there are other circumstances where the connection can be more far-fetched. For example, a news commentator may do a story on a negative event in the region, with bias toward the fact that we should have known this event was to occur.

180. (D) A prototype is an example of a concept. For example, Florida may be considered a prototype for images of sunny places in the United States. It is likely that most people would agree that Florida is a sunny place in the United States.

181. (C) Cognitive schemas are made up of beliefs, assumptions, expectations, and other representations of concepts, places, or things. A cognitive schema is a mental model that we develop based on these factors.

182. (B) Confirmation bias results from assigning more weight to evidence that is in line with one's belief system and minimizing evidence that is less in line with one's belief system. Confirmation bias can cause people to make decisions based more on belief systems than on reasoning.

183. (B) The availability heuristic is a decision-making process that uses the most easily accessible information in one's memory to make decisions, despite the possibility that this information may not be accurate or correct.

184. (E) Sentences are on top of the language hierarchy. They are made up of the phrases (D), which are made up of words (C). Phonemes (A) and morphemes (B) are parts of words.

185. (A) Phonemes are the basic sounds that make up language. Morphemes (B) are not full words but parts of words that contain meanings. Words (C), phrases (D), and sentences (E) use phonemes in order to speak language but do not describe the basic sounds of language.

186. (C) Syntax, sometimes called grammar, is the set of principles of grouping words into phrases and sentences. Syntax is the concept that allows for greater meaning in human language. Noun phrases (A) and verb phrases (B) are formed by syntax guidelines. Linguistic determinism (D) and semantics (E) are not described in the question.

187. (E) At birth human infants are exposed to language and begin to take in sounds, cues, and other ways language is organized. The ability to differentiate sounds and recognize one's language versus other languages occurs at approximately one year of age. Language development continues during the early years.

188. (C) The semantic role of a word is the role it takes in a sentence, impacting the meaning of the sentence. When the same word is in a different role in a sentence, the meaning of the sentence can be quite different.

189. (A) In this case, the use of figurative language (metaphor) evokes a certain thought, thus demonstrating one-way thoughts and language interplay between each other. Although culture has an impact on language (B), this is not specifically demonstrated in the question. The relationships among metaphors, feelings, thoughts, and language, as indicated in the other choices, do exist at times but are not described in the question.

190. (D) Environment has a strong influence on language development. Therefore, children who are not spoken to in their early years have difficulty developing the complex language structures that are second nature to most humans. Although the other choices do influence language and language development, they are not demonstrated when a child lacks early exposure to language.

191. (B) The deep structure of a sentence refers to its underlying meaning. The actual words and phrases in a sentence are its surface structure.

192. (B) The human language is by nature semantic. Semantics is the meaning of words and what is said. Heuristic (A) refers to problem-solving methods, many of which use language but are also cognitive (C).

193. (E) Phonemes are units of sound, and sounds vary across languages. The sound of the rolling *r* is frequently unfamiliar to English speakers. Since sounds of letters make up words, some words are difficult to pronounce when speaking new languages. Phonemes are building blocks for the other units of language that are choices, but these units do not describe sound.

194. (D) The prefix *un-* is a morpheme, as it is the smallest unit of language and it contains meaning. Since *un-* does not stand on its own as a word, it is not a word (C). Phonemes (E) are units of sound. Sentences (A) and phrases (B) contain morphemes.

195. (D) The theory posited by Benjamin Whorf is called the linguistic relativity hypothesis. This theory indicates that language is much more than stringing sounds and words together. Rather, the meaning and the thinking activities are greatly influenced by one's language.

196. (E) Generally, complex language in children develops before age five. Children begin speaking and using some structures of language earlier than age five, but the complex elements do seem to be in place by age five.

197. (A) Whorf's theory explores the ways language impacts thinking. According to linguistic relativity, the ways of thinking about a certain concept do not even come up unless there is some type of language to describe the concept.

198. (D) The expression "she slept like a log" is an example of figurative language. Figurative language is frequently used in American culture to convey ideas. The use of figurative language demonstrates the interplay between thinking and language because the language can conjure up mental images that are different than the literal representation of the language.

Chapter 6: Intelligence

199. (D) Historical intelligence is not one of the multiple intelligences that Howard Gardner theorized about. In addition to musical, linguistic, spatial, and logical-mathematical, Gardner named interpersonal, intrapersonal, bodily kinesthetic, and naturalistic as individual intelligences. Gardner's theory identifies types of intelligence with their own separate and individual capacities. This theory has been challenged.

200. (C) Savant syndrome is characterized by notable talent of an individual in one area, but marked lack of functioning in other areas, often due to the presence of a developmental disability. In this case, Phillip has a diagnosed developmental disability but has the very strong skill of knowing sports statistics.

201. (D) Describing emotions is not a factor in emotional intelligence. The ability to describe emotions may become a factor if the other factors of emotional intelligence exist, but it is not a factor in itself. The other choices are aspects of emotional intelligence.

202. (C) Tacit knowledge involves skill building and how-to skills and is learned from acquiring daily experience. Tacit knowledge is not explicitly learned or taught. Therefore, practical intelligence depends on the tacit knowledge of an individual.

203. (C) Crystallized intelligence is comprised of verbal skills, cognitive skills, and reasoning. Crystallized intelligence influences fluid intelligence (D).

204. (B) Fluid intelligence is the ability to solve emerging issues and use spatial and visual imagery. This includes identifying and using new approaches to problems, as well as quick thinking.

205. (A) The ratio of mental age to chronological age (multiplied by 100) represents the first formula to measure intelligence quotient. Mental age was calculated by developmental place indicated by test scores. This formula was intended for use with children only.

206. (D) Long-term memory is not measured on a Stanford-Binet test. The other factors listed are measured in this type of IQ test. The Stanford-Binet test is only one of the IQ tests used today.

207. (A) Analytical intelligence is typically measured by intelligence tests and is thought to be critical to academic success. The ability for reasoning and problem solving is called practical intelligence (B). The other answer choices represent other types or theories of intelligence.

208. (B) The skills Pauline used include perceiving, managing, using, and understanding emotions. All of these skills are components of emotional intelligence. The other choices refer to other types or theories of intelligence not described in the question.

209. (C) Fluid intelligence includes solving new and emerging issues as well as quick thinking, and it is impacted by fatigue in individuals.

210. (C) The Wechsler Adult Intelligence tests measure verbal and performance abilities. These tests also have additional subsets that measure additional skills (e.g., working memory) related to intelligence.

211. (E) Test-retest reliability is the ability of a test to yield similar results each time it is taken. With intelligence tests, even if tests are taken with years in between, tests that are age appropriate yield similar results over time.

212. (D) The genetic influence of intelligence is not a limitation of the tests themselves. It is an important consideration in the area of intelligence. The other choices indicate known limitations of IQ tests.

213. (B) Access to resources, nutrition, and intellectual stimulation are all environmental factors that influence intelligence. This is an important factor to consider when looking at poverty and intelligence data.

214. (D) There are great differences in the abilities of individuals with mental retardation, but the qualities that indicate mental retardation include less-than-average intelligence and difficulties in adaptive functioning.

215. (B) *Gifted* is the term used to describe an individual with above-average IQ who also shows leadership and creativity. *Genius* (D) is not a term used in psychology but rather in popular culture. Both savant (C) and prodigy (E) indicate extreme excellence in one area, and a savant typically has major deficits as well.

216. (D) Identical twins raised apart show very close correlations of IQ scores. Limitations to this research are that there are not too many cases of identical twins raised apart. Additionally, many times identical twins raised apart are raised in families of similar socioeconomic status. Regardless, this research finding indicates the importance of genetics in intelligence.

217. (B) The cultural environment may overtly and/or covertly focus on skill building in the visual and spatial arenas for men, and men in the American culture are likely to engage in physical and spatially oriented careers. Generally, cultural environment is a critical factor to consider when looking at intelligence differences, as the environmental and genetic interplay in intelligence is repeatedly seen in the research.

218. (B) Predictive validity refers to the ability of a test to measure what it's intended to measure, and in this case is compared with an independent measure (workplace and school success). Choice (A) would indicate that IQ tests have little predictive validity. Choice (C) is an example of test-retest reliability, and choice (E) is an example of split-half reliability.

219. (A) The triarchic theory of intelligence includes analytical, creative, and practical intelligences. Analytical intelligence is the ability to solve problems and learn new things. Creative intelligence is the ability to adjust to new situations. Practical intelligence includes the ability to solve problems.

220. (B) Toby displays all of the qualities of emotional intelligence. Awareness of one's own emotions, the emotions of others, and the impact of emotions on one's life is an important quality not measured by intelligence tests.

221. (C) The Wechsler Adult Intelligence Scale–Third Edition (WAIS-III) measures verbal abilities and perceptual skills. The Stanford-Binet intelligence test (A) measures some of the other qualities. Since performance tests (D) do not rely on language, they do not measure verbal abilities.

222. (D) Performance tests are intelligence tests that do not rely on language. They are sometimes used with preverbal children, individuals with mental retardation, or those without English-language skills. Culture-fair tests (E) attempt to limit culture bias but may still be written and rely on language skills.

223. (C) The question describes an individual with savant syndrome. Savant syndrome is characterized by high performance in one particular arena but also lower than average intelligence (mental retardation).

Chapter 7: Motivation and Emotion

224. (C) A motive is a need or desire that incites goal-directed behavior. Feelings (A) and emotions (E) can influence or be influenced by behavior (D). A drive (B) is an internal state of arousal that is caused by internal bodily needs and can incite motivation.

225. (C) Homeostasis is the internal sense of balance that an individual seeks. The process of homeostasis can involve various internal processes. One effort toward achieving homeostasis is maintaining body temperature, or thermoregulation (E).

226. (B) Drive-reduction theory states that drives arise from a change in homeostasis, and individuals seek to return to homeostasis through goal-oriented behaviors.

227. (C) The root of motivation in arousal theory is to reach optimum arousal. The optimum level of arousal can change related to the moment. Different types of tasks appear to require different levels of arousal.

228. (C) Incentives are external stimuli that provoke behavior. The key word here is *external*, as many of the other choices indicate internal human processes. In the case of incentives, an individual is exposed to an outside experience that incites a behavior.

229. (C) Extrinsic motivation is one where behavior is induced due to an award or punishment structure. In this case the salesman is motivated because of the bonus award. Although purposely working more and selling more can be considered a goal-directed behavior, *goal-directed motivation* is not a term in the motivational theory.

230. (D) Thirst can be triggered by both internal and external cues. External cues like walking by a water fountain (C) and seeing a commercial for water (E) provide direct links to thirst. Time of day is more likely an external cultural cue for hunger but not necessarily thirst.

231. (D) Sex is considered the socially oriented human motivation. Although there are ways to achieve sexual orgasm through nonsocial ways (e.g., masturbation), the duality of sexual hormones, organs, and the motivation for mate choices indicate the social orientation of sex.

232. (E) The pituitary gland is located near the hypothalamus, one of the primary structures involved in regulating hunger, but it is not directly involved in regulating eating and hunger. There are many different physiological structures and qualities that influence hunger and eating.

233. (A) Arousal theory states that people are motivated by finding the optimal arousal level, whereas the drive-reduction theory states that people are motivated to reduce a drive and return to homeostasis. Both of these theories are theories of motivation.

234. (B) According to Yerkes-Dodson law, maximizing performance on complicated tasks requires lower arousal, while maximizing performance on simple tasks requires higher arousal levels.

235. (E) An incentive is an external stimulus that prompts some sort of goal-directed behavior. In this case, the behavior is visiting the restaurant, and the stimulus is the advertisement. These factors make up an incentive.

236. (B) Chloe is showing intrinsic motivation in this example. Intrinsic motivation originates internally, making the motivation for the behavior the behavior itself. In the case of Chloe playing, there are no external factors that drive the behavior.

237. (D) A secondary drive is a drive that is learned, whereas hunger is physiological and not learned, making it a primary drive. The other choices, cultural (A), biological (B), environmental (C), and psychological (E) factors do impact eating behaviors in individuals.

238. (D) Our memory, or lack of memory, of our last meal is related to our short-term, or possibly long-term, memory abilities. Those with short-term memory deficits may have difficulty remembering their last meal and, therefore, experience some misguided cues around if they are in fact hungry. This phenomenon is not influenced by culture, but the other choices are impacted by culture.

239. (B) Unlike other organisms, much of human sexual behavior is learned. This is demonstrated by the fact that individuals continue to engage in sexual behavior after hormone levels or presence has changed. Choices (A) and (E) describe qualities of nonhuman sexual behavior, while choices (C) and (D) are present in human and non-human sexual behavior.

240. (B) Excitement is the first phase of human sexual response, and it's followed by the plateau phase with increasing arousal but at a slower pace. Orgasm follows the plateau phase, after which both males and females move to resolution, or return to previous heart rates and muscle relaxation.

241. (E) Culture is definitely a factor in aggression and the way aggressive behaviors are expressed in humans. Some argue that the exposure to violent media increases aggression. Cultural differences in aggressive behaviors exist regionally in the United States, by religious backgrounds, and in many other cultural contexts.

242. (C) Although motivations or behaviors may be driven by emotions, or in turn may influence emotions, emotions themselves are not motivations. The other choices do describe specific motivations frequently found in humans.

243. (A) Self-actualization is at the top of Maslow's hierarchy and refers to a realization of potential in an individual. According to Maslow's theory, an individual can only begin the process of reaching his or her own best potential after other needs in the hierarchy are met.

244. (B) Safety needs include shelter, health, and other basic needs above food and water. In this case, Natalie needs to fulfill her safety needs before moving up the hierarchy to belongingness needs.

245. (D) There are many different definitions of the word *emotions*. Emotions are affective responses. They are related to the way we feel and the influences on our behaviors and physiology of our feeling states. Intelligence is not a part of the definition of *emotions*, but level of emotional intelligence, or EQ score, may impact expression or handling of emotions.

246. (C) Pain is not one of Plutchik's basic emotions. Pain may be related to sadness for some, but it can describe both physical and emotional pain.

247. (B) Display rules dictate through cultural norms the way emotions are expressed. Display rules are also in play when people are encouraged to express certain emotions in particular social settings. Perception of emotions (A) has been shown as similar across cultures. Mood states (D) and affective responses (E) are related to emotions but not to display rules.

248. (A) The James-Lange theory states that the experience of emotion is dictated by the experience of the physiological changes. It is the physiological changes and an individual's awareness of those changes that prompt emotional responses.

249. (B) The Cannon-Bard theory of emotions states that emotional and physiological changes are triggered simultaneously in response to environmental stimuli. This theory does not attempt to distinguish which response comes first, as there is a belief that emotions and physiological changes impact each other as soon as the stimuli is presented.

Chapter 8: Social Psychology

250. (C) Social psychology is the study of how an individual's thoughts, feelings, and behaviors are influenced by the actions and qualities of others. The actions and qualities of others may be real or inferred by the individual, but are nonetheless strong forces in the social universe.

251. (D) Attributions are inferences about why people behave in the way they do. In this case, Carla has made an inference or a judgment about why her interviewee is behaving nervously, maybe because he really wants the job or being on the spot in the interview process is not comfortable for him. Regardless of what the inference is about the behavior, that inference is called an attribution.

252. (B) The primacy effect is the concept that early data about an individual can carry more influence than later data about the individual. This may influence the cultural emphasis in the United States on making good first impressions.

253. (B) Schemata allow for the organization of information into categories, and they influence how individuals interpret and remember information. Schemata include preconceived notions about the world and about individuals. Our schemata can be both conscious and subconscious and can have both positive and negative impacts on our thinking and perceptions.

254. (B) A fundamental attribution error involves incorrectly identifying the source of behavior as internally motivated or as a result of internal qualities without considering the possible external or situational qualities that could impact the situation.

255. (B) Thoughts, feelings, and behaviors toward someone, something, or another factor make up one's attitude. Attitudes can trigger emotional responses and are sometimes guided by motivation.

256. (E) A self-fulfilling prophecy is typically based on a stereotype (D) but is not a stereotype itself. A self-fulfilling prophecy is a person's beliefs or expectations about another that increase the possibility that the expectations will occur. In other words, beliefs about behavior may elicit the expected behavior.

257. (B) This is a just-world attribution error. A just-world attribution error is one based on the assumption that only bad things happen to bad people and only good things happen to good people. In this case, a bad thing happened to Julie. It was very difficult for her, as she had believed that as a good person only good things would happen to her.

258. (A) This is called stereotyping and is the result of schemas about certain groups. Stereotyping can result in judgments about other people. Stereotyping can cause problems for individuals as well as communities and the world at large.

259. (A) Mr. Palmer has made an inference about the "showing-off" behavior of his son Corey. An inference about the cause for behaviors is called an attribution.

260. (B) The question describes a defensive attribution error. Defensive attribution errors are those that attribute personal qualities and efforts to successes, while attributing social and external qualities to failures.

261. (D) Trust is a factor in love and can be built up over time, but it is not a factor in initial attraction. Physical attractiveness (A) has been linked to attractiveness, as has physical proximity, including where people reside (C). Similarity (B) can be a factor in many arenas, including interests and values. Equitable exchanges (E) with the other play a factor in attractiveness.

262. (B) Culture has a great influence on the way that people behave; therefore, it can play a large part in attribution. For example, people from different cultural backgrounds may have different beliefs about the role of family and the role of work, and may also have different social mores around family gatherings. All of these factors play a part in attribution.

263. (A) Choice (A) describes a fundamental attribution error, which is attributing a certain behavior to internal qualities without considering the possible external circumstances surrounding the situation. The other choices describe errors but do not specifically describe a fundamental attribution error.

264. (B) The primacy effect describes the tendency to give more weight to first impression data rather than later data when forming impressions about people. Although it may be referred to causally as a *first impression error* (E), this is not a term used in psychology.

265. (C) Stereotypes are a result of negative schemata or categorizations of people in groups with negative connotations. Prejudices (A) result from stereotyping but refer to attitudes toward others rather than the categorizations and beliefs.

266. (C) This example describes a defensive attribution error because Cameron attributes success to internal qualities and failure to external qualities. "Failure" is not earning first place, which for many is not considered failure. Regardless, the lack of self-ownership and the attribution of the results to solely external factors make this a defensive attribution error.

267. (B) The tendency to assume that bad things happen to bad people is called the just-world hypothesis. Although it may sound like it is a *culturally biased attribution error* (C), that is not a term used in the psychological literature, nor is it a judgment attribution error (E).

268. (A) This phenomena is called out-group homogeneity. The individual is not part of the group, thus it is an "out-group" rather than an "in-group." The term *homogeneity* refers to the sameness of the group. A group may have some homogeneous qualities, for example, members of the same race, but individuals in this group do not necessarily share other similar qualities. Therefore, out-group homogeneity is a type of stereotyping.

269. (B) The discomfort caused by an inconsistency or contradiction between actions and attitudes is called cognitive dissonance. The desire in individuals to decrease cognitive dissonance is a form of self-persuasion.

270. (E) Scores on intelligence tests are not a direct factor in attitudes. The way an individual interprets his or her scores may be a factor of some sort, but the scores themselves are not a factor. The other choices are factors that can and do influence attitudes.

271. (B) A high self-monitor is likely to act more on perceived expectations rather than his or her own attitudes, making behavior more difficult to predict. Low self-monitors (A), on the other hand, demonstrate and act on their attitudes more frequently, making behavior easier to predict.

272. (C) The frustration-aggression theory of prejudice states that one of the roots of prejudice is frustration in meeting personal goals that leads to anger or aggression toward a less powerful target. The target of this individual's anger is affirmative action policies, which in turn has prejudicial implications. In reality, the job market, the economic outlook, and the person's interviewing skills and workplace experience may all impact his or her ability to gain employment.

273. (B) The peripheral route to persuasion is not rooted in a deep cognitive process but rather more superficial qualities. In this case, the attractiveness and charisma of the candidate persuades the voter. This type of persuasion is more common around issues that are of less importance or value to the individual.

274. (E) The discrepancy between her beliefs about health and her smoking habit cause a cognitive dissonance for Tina. This state is one that Tina could mitigate through persuading herself to change, by either changing her attitudes about health and life-style, or by changing her smoking behaviors.

275. (C) Schema is not a function of persuasion in the communication model. That said, schema influences attitudes and likely influences how/if/when one changes one's attitude. However, according to the communication model of persuasion, the message, source of the message, the way in which it's delivered, and the characteristics of the audience all influence persuasion.

276. (A) Although uncovering underlying prejudices through empirical studies may be a way of identifying unknown prejudices, it does not provide a specific way to reduce prejudices. The other choices are specific strategies toward reducing individual prejudices.

277. (A) High self-monitors tend to attempt to assess the expectations of others and behave according to the perceived expectations. Low self-monitors tend to act according to their attitudes more consistently.

278. (D) A series of acts that limits access to social capital and opportunities to groups or members of particular groups is considered discrimination. Discrimination is often based on prejudice (B) and stereotyping (A). Prejudice is the attitude; stereotype is the schema or believed characteristics of a certain group; discrimination is the action.

279. (E) Conformity involves a change in behaviors, and sometimes attitudes, based on perceived social expectations. In this case, individuals may begin to question their own answers when they hear others' answers. Or they do not want to stick out with a different answer, so they may choose answers closer to the majority rather than their own answers.

280. (D) Cognitive dissonance is not a specific type of social influence and is based on a disconnect between individual attitudes and behaviors. Social influences include conformity (A), obedience (B), compliance (C), and group dynamics (E).

281. (B) The question describes a change in typical behavior for Kristie and is a response to a directive from someone else, making it an experience of obedience. The other choices are other types of social influences but are not obedience.

282. (D) The door-in-the-face technique involves expecting the initial request to be turned down in order to open the door for a more reasonable request. In this case, the technique is used in the hopes that the donor will comply with a request below the initial high request.

283. (C) The bystander effect is in play when no one from a large group acts to provide help to an individual in distress. Generally, the larger the group is, the less likely it is that someone will provide help.

284. (B) Social facilitation involves the tendency for individuals to perform better on tasks when in the presence of other people. In this case, although the coach is tracking individual times, instructing student athletes to run against each other in order to track the times likely increases their speed in the time trials.

285. (D) It is likely that Derek had an experience of deindividuation, in which his personal responsibility was diminished and his anonymity was increased. This led Derek to behave in way that he would not have otherwise.

286. (C) In situations with high group cohesiveness, a pattern of thinking known as groupthink can lead to flawed decision making. When this occurs, the group tends to agree on decision making but without attention to different arguments or points of view.

287. (A) Group polarization is characterized by a shift toward a more extreme stance after a group discussion. This can occur even if the discussion was intended to move the group toward alignment.

288. (D) Social loafing is the phenomenon of group process that involves the tendency of individuals to produce less effort when part of a group. It appears that individual motivation and effort are impacted by participation in a group.

289. (B) Milgram's study was on obedience. Despite the distress of the students ("teachers" in the study) and the perceived distress of the "learners," students continued to apply increased electric shocks as that was the instruction of the study leaders. The learners were in fact actors and were not truly receiving a shock, but the perception of the shocks was quite real. Results in the field of obedience from this study have had widespread implications on the field.

290. (B) Collectivist cultures are those that tend to place greater value on the good of the group than on the individual. Because of this value, conformity to social norms of the group is generally higher than in other types of cultures.

291. (E) Altruism is a helping behavior without motivation toward self-gain or rewards. The focus of the helping from an altruistic point of view is the other. The expectation of altruistic behaviors varies across cultures.

292. (B) As the number of individuals in a group increases, the likelihood that an individual helps someone in distress decreases. This is called the bystander effect. This behavior may be linked to a decreased belief in responsibility or a belief that someone else will help the individual in distress.

293. (A) The Hawthorne effect ascertains that the presence of researchers, or participants' knowledge of their inclusion in the research, can impact productivity or behavior. This phenomenon is important in social psychology as it points out the strong impact of others' presence related to outcomes.

294. (C) The bystander effect is in play when no one from a large group acts to provide help to an individual in distress. Generally, the larger the group is, the less likely it is that someone will provide help. On a busy road, some may believe that with all of the passing cars another car will stop to help.

295. (E) What people say about their feelings is only one part of the way feelings are expressed. Body language, including facial expressions and posture, can also provide valuable data. The way someone storms off or comes close to another provides information about how people are feeling.

Chapter 9: Development

296. (A) The embryonic stage occurs after the zygote attaches to the uterine wall and continues until the fetal stage. The fetal stage occurs at approximately the ninth week until birth.

297. (D) The placenta plays many roles in the developing fetus, but temperature regulation is not one of them. The other choices are roles of the placenta.

298. (D) Teratogens are environmental substances or conditions that negatively impact fetal development. Teratogens can be ingested by a mother or can be a result of exposure.

299. (E) A small head circumference, not a large head circumference, is a symptom of fetal alcohol syndrome. The other choices do describe symptoms of fetal alcohol syndrome. Symptoms of fetal alcohol syndrome are expressed differently on a case-by-case basis, but the cluster of certain symptoms assists in the diagnosis.

300. (D) Newborns cry but crying is not a reflex. Crying is a state expressed by newborns, and sometimes crying is an attempt to communicate needs. Reflexes involve controlled responses of body movements.

301. (B) An infant's patterns of behavior, emotion, and self-regulation are considered his or her temperament. Temperament is thought to be largely genetically determined, as temperament is expressed in utero as well as in early infancy.

302. (C) The child in this question displays object permanence. The child searches for a toy that he or she cannot see, thus demonstrating awareness that objects do exist even when they are no longer in plain sight. If this child did not have the ability of object permanence, the child would not search for something completely out of sight.

303. (E) This child is demonstrating assimilation. Assimilation involves using current schemes, or ways in which one organizes the world, in order to interpret new information. This child had already learned what a kitty was, and when he saw a tiger toy he automatically associated it with a kitty.

304. (C) The question describes a difficult child as defined by Thomas and Chess's (1984) temperament research. The shy child temperament was added after additional temperament research.

305. (C) Prenatal vitamins are frequently recommended and are known to positively impact fetal development. Teratogens negatively impact fetal development. Generally, expectant mothers are exposed to teratogens purposely (in the case of drinking alcohol) or inadvertently (in the case of air pollution, x-rays, and exposure to measles).

306. (E) This infant is displaying the rooting reflex. Rooting is a precursor to sucking (A) but involves searching with one's mouth for the sucking object. Rooting is an important reflex involved in breast-feeding.

307. (C) Infants with slow-to-warm-up temperament display low interest in new activities and experiences and low reactivity to the experiences once they are engaged. The other choices incorrectly identify the interest and reactivity levels of this type of infant.

308. (A) Children from birth until age two are in the sensory-motor stage, and it is during this period that children develop object permanence. Object permanence is the understanding that objects exist even if they are out of sight.

309. (E) A 10-year-old who cleans his room in order to earn video game time is behaving in a particular way in order to earn a reward. Behavior motivated by earning a reward or avoiding punishment typically takes place during the preconventional stage according to Kohlberg's theory. The preconventional stage is thought to occur in pre-adolescence; therefore, the age of the boy in this question provides another clue.

310. (B) A child demonstrates egocentric thinking in the preoperational stage. This means that a child thinks only from his or her point of view and is unable to consider the point of view of others.

311. (B) Piaget's formal operational stage is characterized in part by abstract thinking, while the concrete operational stage is characterized by concrete thinking. Egocentric thinking and viewpoints are present in the preoperational stage, which is before both the concrete operational and formal operational stages.

312. (D) Piaget did present empirical data to back up his findings. Some of the data include observations of children. The other choices are criticisms of Piaget's theory. Despite the criticisms Piaget did lay some groundwork for the field of cognitive development.

313. (E) A longitudinal study is limited by the use of time and resources, participant attrition, and the ability to identify the reasons for the differences as primarily developmental. Because a longitudinal study follows the same cohort over time, participant group differences are not an issue.

314. (C) According to Bowlby, a secure base is one with which an infant or child can explore the world. A child with a secure base can explore his or her surroundings and then return to the parent. Variations in attachment develop in part due to the quality or presence of a secure base.

315. (B) Imprinting is a learning process that is seen in many animal species. Because the first moving object an animal sees is most likely its mother, imprinting allows for attachment and learning from the mother. At times animals have been known to attach to species or objects that are not their mothers but do tend to continue to follow and take cues from that object.

316. (B) An authoritarian parenting style is characterized by expectations of strict obedience and demands, with a lower level of responsiveness. This parenting style is not associated with positive outcomes for children, and children can have difficulty with communicating and trusting others.

317. (B) Parallel play is characterized by toddlers playing side by side but not together. Toddlers engaged in this type of play may look at each other or investigate what the other is doing, but they do not play together. This is an expected stage in childhood development.

318. (D) Generally children say their first word at about one year of age. Not until later will the word be used in a sentence or be strung with other words. Before saying their first word, infants will babble and use sounds to communicate and become familiar with their voices.

319. (E) According to Erikson, the first stage of psychosocial development is trust versus mistrust, and it occurs from infancy to approximately 18 months. Trust is built with caregiver reliability and attention, allowing a child to trust that the caregiver will take good care of him or her. Mistrust can occur in circumstances with neglectful, abusive, or disorganized caregivers.

320. (A) Mental stimulation is a key nonmedical factor related to sustained cognitive functioning in older adulthood. Two of the choices, biological predisposition for Alzheimer's disease (B) and circulatory decline (D) are medical factors associated with cognitive functioning. Although social capital (E) can influence mental stimulation, mental stimulation does not need to be social.

321. (C) Smell, hearing, and sight tend to decline with old age. These changed sensory experiences can drastically change the way one operates in the world. For example, driving skills and ability to live alone can be impacted with declines in sight, hearing, and smell.

322. (D) By engaging in social referencing, infants gain information about their surroundings. The process of social referencing demonstrates that infants engage in their social world very early on. The other choices are also social-related behaviors of infants, but they do not specifically refer to using facial expressions to gain information.

323. (A) A permissive-independent parenting style is associated with dependent or needy children. A permissive-indulgent parenting style is associated with impulsive children. There are many other qualities of children who are raised in these types of parenting styles, as well as different qualities associated with different parenting styles.

324. (E) Menarche is the first menstrual period experienced by girls who are in puberty. This occurs many years past the age of three. The other choices do occur at approximately three years of age. It is important to use "approximately" when referring to developmental milestones, as many do not occur at fixed moments in time.

325. (B) Young children, especially before they become school aged, can negatively impact the reports of marital satisfaction. This may be due to the increased pressures, changed roles and responsibilities, and divided attention brought into the family with the arrival of a baby. Although marital dissatisfaction may be at its highest when raising teenagers, it does tend to bounce back as children get older.

326. (D) Stress is not a stage of dying according to Kübler-Ross's five stages of dying. That is not to say that those dying will not experience stress. Many times one will experience high stress. The other choices are part of Kübler-Ross's model, as is depression. Theses stages are not linear; people may pass through each stage differently and also return to previous stages.

327. (B) Identity versus role confusion occurs during adolescence and is greatly impacted by peer relationships. During this phase teens attempt to develop a sense of self, and this occurs with the help of peer and other social relationships.

328. (B) Authoritarian parenting is associated with children who are socially responsible and self-sufficient. This parenting style includes setting firm boundaries but also listening to children and clarifying parental decisions.

329. (C) Temperament is thought to be inborn or developed very early on in infants. Temperament may be related to how or why some children are accepted or rejected in peer circles. For example, his or her peers may not accept a child with a difficult temperament. Children gain social and emotional support (A and B), learn problem-solving abilities (D), and have positive play experiences (E) within peer relationships.

330. (C) Testes growth is a primary sexual characteristic that occurs during puberty. It is considered primary because the growth of the testes is directly involved in reproduction. Facial hair growth, a secondary sexual characteristic, occurs during puberty and indicates sexual maturity but is not involved in reproduction.

331. (A) Adolescence is correlated with increased depression for individuals. The issues around self-esteem and self-image that emerge during this time can cause quite challenging feelings for young people. Because of the increased levels of depression as well as rates of suicide, it is important to pay attention to what is happening with youth during this period.

332. (D) Bonding exclusively with caregivers is not a quality of the adolescent experience. In fact, bonding with peers is more present during adolescence, and adolescents may in fact seek increased privacy and distance from parents.

333. (C) Industry versus inferiority occurs during school-aged years. During this stage children develop school-based skills, social skills, and physical agility skills. Generativity versus stagnation occurs in middle-aged years, when an individual has developed a life path of some sort and fulfills goals that he or she had set out to fulfill. Failure to meet the goals of either stage can lead to difficult feelings and experiences of the world.

Chapter 10: Personality

334. (D) Although thoughts may influence personality, cognition is not a part of the Big Five personality traits. Agreeableness is the other personality dimension in the Big Five not listed in these choices.

335. (B) Traits are considered relatively stable patterns of behaving, thinking, and feeling. People tend to display their traits across situations. For example, someone who is generally calm may display calmness at school, at work, and with friends.

336. (C) Psychodynamic theories focus on experiences outside of consciousness. One example is defense mechanisms. There is also a lens toward early childhood experiences in these types of theories.

337. (B) The id is the "pleasure principle." Therefore, one who is guided only by pleasure could be seen as having an overdeveloped id. The id is thought to be the first structure to develop, with the ego and superego developing after the id.

338. (E) Carl Jung, the founder of Jungian theory, identified the collective unconscious as shared images and stories that are present in all human beings. These images and stories are inherited and not based on individual experiences.

339. (A) Confused is not a pattern of attachment. The other choices are patterns of attachment that have been well researched and written about in the literature. Patterns of attachment are thought to influence the way people interact in relationships.

340. (C) Erik Erikson is responsible for identifying stages of development. Progress through the stages does have a large impact on personality and especially one's sense of self.

341. (B) The self-actualization tendency states that people are driven toward reaching their potential. According to Rogers, those who reach their inborn potential are considered fully functioning and self-actualized.

342. (C) Positive psychology generally focuses on factors that make people happy rather than paying attention to problems or difficulties. Positive psychology focuses on both positive traits and positive states.

343. (A) Psychodynamic theory has a strong focus on the unconscious and on the unconscious patterns that contribute to our roles in relationships. Sometimes these unconscious factors are driven by defense mechanisms and sexual and aggressive urges.

344. (C) The superego guides moral behavior according to Freudian theory. This is the last aspect of the personality structure to develop. The superego includes guidelines that are internalized from the social universe.

345. (B) The ego is known as the "reality principle" of the personality, and it mediates between the id and superego. The id is known as the "pleasure principle," and the superego is known as the conscious or "moral principle."

346. (E) Humanism, or humanistic theory, is rooted in the belief of human good and the inborn drive to strive toward self-actualization. Unconditional positive regard is the acceptance of another despite his or her behaviors or actions.

347. (D) The latency stage of the psychosexual development is characterized by no interest in the opposite sex. According to Freudian theory, it occurs between approximately age 5 and approximately age 12.

348. (C) Generally, Freudian theory states that defense mechanisms are created in order to protect the ego from the anxiety created during an inability to regulate id drives and the moral ideal of the superego. Defense mechanisms can serve to protect the ego in certain ways but not regarding criticism from others.

349. (B) The superego represents internalized standards of morality and conscious. Because of this, if the ego attempts to regulate needs of the id with expectations of the superego and does not live up to the superego, guilt may ensue. An individual may experience guilt that he or she did not behave according to what his or her superego expected.

350. (B) Repression is the defense mechanism used to exclude difficult memories or feelings from consciousness. Defense mechanisms are unconscious strategies to protect the ego or lessen anxiety.

351. (B) For Erikson, the parent-child relationship quality is a key factor in personality development. This relationship allows a child to progress through the eight stages of development. For Rogers, the search for self-actualization, as well as the belief in human good, are key factors in personality development.

352. (C) A tenet of Horney's theory is the motivating factor of anxiety. Anxiety is a reaction to threats that are real or imagined, and people develop strategies of coping that are then seen in personality styles.

353. (A) Introverts are thought to be mainly concerned with their own internal private worlds, while extroverts are concerned with the social universe. The concepts of introvert and extrovert come from Jungian theory.

354. (B) Reaction formation is a defense mechanism characterized by an outward expression of feelings or emotions that are opposite from the internal feelings of an individual. In this case, the individual expresses and in ways consciously believes the negative feelings about homosexuality as a way to deal with his or her internal homosexual feelings.

355. (E) According to Freudian theory the Oedipal complex is young boys' attraction and attachment to their mothers and, therefore, jealousy toward their fathers. On the other hand, the Electra complex is experienced by young girls and is jealousy of the mother and intense attraction and attachment to the father.

356. (C) Psychodynamic thought does have an emphasis on human relationships. There is evidence that relationships are important and that patterns of relationships play out in many parts of peoples lives. The other choices are criticisms of psychodynamic theories.

357. (C) The concept of the collective unconscious comes from Jungian theory. The collective unconscious is shared across individuals and cultures according to the theory. The collective unconscious includes shared mental images.

358. (D) Object relations and ego psychology are considered psychodynamic theories. These theories have some focus on the unconscious patterns of relating and thinking. Ego psychology focuses on the functioning of the ego. The focus of object relations is on self and objects, which are typically other individuals or objects that make up mental representations for others.

359. (C) The unconscious is not a part of the social-cognitive approach to personality. The hallmarks of the social-cognitive approach include cognitions (A), past experiences (B), learning (D), and the experience in the social universe (E).

360. (B) An internal locus of control indicates a belief that the individual can control one's fate by one's actions. One with a high internal locus of control may behave in ways that are internally motivating and not leave circumstances up to chance.

361. (E) Many aspects of the cognitive-social approaches are testable, as are the therapies that have emerged from these theories. Testable approaches can lead to increased understanding of psychological treatments.

362. (C) The MMPI, a widely used personality assessment, is a self-report objective test. Although it is easy to score, the self-report nature of the test does leave room for testing errors.

363. (C) The concept of self-efficacy involves an individual's belief in one's abilities to accomplish certain things and the influence of these beliefs on one's behaviors. An individual with high self-efficacy may try more options to succeed in a task because of his or her belief in his or her abilities to accomplish the task.

364. (D) This client demonstrates having an external locus of control. The client displays a belief that the circumstances he or she is experiencing are beyond control and others, or other external circumstances, are ultimately in control.

365. (B) A cognitive-social approach is centered around individual experiences, thoughts and feelings about self and the experiences, and beliefs about the amount of control one has around the experiences. Learning is also an important construct in a cognitive-social approach, and much of learning comes from experiences.

366. (D) The key assessment tool in a Rorschach test is preconceived inkblots that people are asked to react to. Psychodynamically oriented psychologists use this tool more often than other psychologists. Reliability, validity, and overall usage of the Rorschach have been frequently questioned, but regardless it is a key assessment tool in the field of psychology.

367. (D) An individual's level of achievement orientation is related to conscientiousness, rather than neuroticism. The other choices are related to neuroticism.

Chapter 11: Psychopathology

368. (D) The somatogenic hypothesis of mental disorders found mental disorders to be rooted organically or in the body of individuals. Similarly, the biological model sees mental disorders as being based in biochemical or physiological bases.

369. (B) Symptoms are reported by the patient. Examples of symptoms include lack of appetite, sadness, or nerves. Signs are observed by the clinician. Examples of signs include body tension, anxious affect, or minimal eye contact.

370. (D) With the emergence of DSM diagnosis and, therefore, categorizing psychological disorders came the ability to study and treat people with similar conditions when outcomes were positive. Empirical studies of psychological treatments often include specific diagnostic categories. The other choices list criticisms of the DSM and of psychological diagnosing in general.

371. (D) The definition of mental disorders does not include a biological origin. That said, some mental disorders are believed to be biologically based. The other choices are aspects of the definition.

372. (E) Compulsions are characterized by behaviors that are repetitive and, at times, ritualistic in nature. In this case, the young woman is demonstrating repetitive behavior around hand washing.

373. (B) Symptoms of posttraumatic stress disorder are generally in these three categories: hyperarousal, avoidance, and re-experiencing. An example of re-experiencing is flashbacks. An example of hyperarousal is experiencing increased heart rate at the thought of the incident or the conglomerate of incidents. An example of avoidance is an attempt to avoid all things that provide any reminder of the incident or incidents.

374. (A) Generalized anxiety disorder is characterized by frequent and free-floating worry. People who experience generalized anxiety disorder may worry about one thing, and once that is resolved they may worry about the next thing. Sometimes these worries can be around personal or a loved one's safety, perception of competency, or general overarching things.

375. (C) Decreased need for sleep, pressured speech, grandiose thoughts, and impaired judgment (including excessive spending) are associated with mania. Terry's roommate may be having a manic episode. Manic episodes are associated with bipolar disorder.

376. (C) Euphoric feelings are feelings of elatedness. These feelings are not associated with depression. The other choices are associated with depression.

377. (B) The basis of the diathesis-stress model of psychological disorders is the biological predisposition to psychological disorders that is then activated by stressors. In this case, the teenage boy may have a biological predisposition to psychosis that was not uncovered until the stress of divorce allowed it to emerge.

378. (D) Axis IV is where social and environmental problems are listed. For example, difficulties with occupation, finances, housing, and other social circumstances may be listed. At times, clinicians assess severity of these symptoms by noting mild, moderate, or severe or by using other rating scales.

379. (E) Bipolar disorder is characterized by states of depressed mood and of mania. The question describes some symptoms of depressed mood (sadness, hopelessness, low mood) and mania (euphoria, racing thoughts, pressured speech), but both of these states can have other symptoms as well.

380. (C) Anxiety disorders are characterized by intense worry or discomfort. Those suffering from anxiety disorders may avoid certain situations or let their behavior be guided by avoiding or limiting the discomfort.

381. (D) Obsessions are disturbing thoughts that are frequent and recurrent. Obsessive thoughts frequently lead to compulsive behaviors.

382. (B) Cognitive distortions are distorted views of self or the world, likely based on early childhood experiences, that influence the way one thinks about oneself and acts in the world. Cognitive distortions include things like catastrophizing and discounting the positive factors of oneself. All-or-nothing thinking (E) is also an example of a cognitive distortion.

383. (A) Men tend to use methods that are more lethal when attempting suicide. For example, men may use guns or jumping methods, while women may use pill overdoses that are less likely to be successful. Women are statistically more likely to attempt suicide, but men are statistically more likely to complete suicide.

384. (C) The SCID, Structured Clinical Interview for Diagnosis, is a semistructured interview that leads the clinician and interviewee through a number of questions geared around the *Diagnostic and Statistical Manual of Mental Disorders* diagnoses.

385. (C) Systems theory, sometimes called the biopsychosocial approach, is one that includes a biological, social, and psychological lens toward mental disorders. This is an inclusive approach that considers many aspects of human functioning and can assist in explaining why some people in the same circumstances have vastly different psychological outcomes.

386. (C) Signs are what the patient displays and are observed by the psychologist. In this case, nothing that is noted by the psychologist is about what the patient describes. Rather the notes are the psychologist's observations about the patient's condition. Therefore, the psychologist is describing signs in the notes.

387. (A) Axis I is where current psychological disorders are listed. Individuals often seek treatment for Axis I disorders. Personality disorders and mental retardation are mental disorders that are not diagnosed on Axis II (B).

388. (C) *Insane*, or *insanity*, is a word from the legal profession that is sometimes used by the general population, but psychologists do not use this word. Psychologists use clinical terms that appropriately describe people's conditions. For example, psychologists typically do not use *schizophrenic* (D) to describe a person. Instead, they may use the phrase "individual with schizophrenia."

389. (B) Dysthymia is characterized by a long period of low-level depression. It is not as severe as a major depressive disorder (A), but it may last much longer. Mania (E) and hypomania (D) are symptoms of bipolar disorder (C), which is also a mood disorder.

390. (C) Concentration and memory impairment are cognitive symptoms, which means they are related to thought and brain functioning. Although some other symptoms may be organic and treated by medication, concentration and memory impairment are specifically cognitive.

391. (E) An individual with bipolar disorder is at higher risk for suicide than one with any other disorder. Although the data change, approximately 20 percent of individuals with bipolar disorder commit suicide, and many more than that attempt suicide.

392. (B) In some cases, depression is thought to arise from a lack of serotonin in the synaptic cleft. Therefore, Selective Serotonin Reuptake Inhibitors (SSRIs), also called antidepressants, seek to keep serotonin in the synaptic cleft. Generally, serotonin is the neurotransmitter most frequently associated with depression, although other neurotransmitters are sometimes associated with depression.

393. (A) A delusion is a false belief. Delusions are at times persecutory, as in this case where an individual believes he or she is being followed. Delusions of grandeur are false beliefs of one's status or power.

394. (C) Excessive amounts of dopamine are associated with psychosis. Schizophrenia is also associated with psychosis.

395. (C) Although symptoms of schizophrenia are sometimes more active in individuals than at other times, there is not a subtype called recurrent schizophrenia. All of the subtypes of schizophrenia have different symptom presentations that fall under the larger category of schizophrenia.

396. (B) Schizoid, antisocial, and borderline are examples of personality disorders. The current version of the *Diagnostic and Statistical Manual of Mental Disorders* includes 10 personality disorders, but this is likely to change in future versions. Because they are believed to be pervasive, personality disorders are not diagnosed on the same axis as other clinical conditions.

397. (D) Social supports are actually a protective factor regarding mood disorders. The quality of relationships can play a part if people develop mood disorders. Additionally, social supports can assist people in getting access to care if they need it, and they can help people when initial warning signs develop.

398. (B) Anxiety disorders are the most common mental disorder in the United States. There are many types of anxiety disorders, and some are more common than others.

399. (E) Both hallucinations and delusions are considered positive symptoms of schizophrenia. Positive symptoms are those symptoms that are in excess to one's typical functioning. For example, a delusion is an additional symptom that an individual experiences. Negative symptoms are areas of functioning that one with schizophrenia lacks. For example, an individual with schizophrenia may lack the desire for social interaction.

400. (D) Autism is diagnosed in childhood but does persevere throughout adulthood. Individuals with autism display deficiencies in behavior, communication, and socialization. Autism is a spectrum-based disorder, meaning there are many different levels of functioning and symptom presentation within the autism diagnosis.

401. (A) This particular young adult female appears to be experiencing attention-deficit/hyperactivity disorder (ADHD), which is characterized by inattention and impulsivity. Individuals who experience ADHD often do not perform to their potential due to the attention issues.

402. (B) Agoraphobia is an experience of intense fear around situations in public, crowds, or circumstances that involve a loss of a security of some sort. This fear is often accompanied by panic attacks. Those who experience this kind of panic attack may feel safe and secure only at home. Therefore, they spend most to all of their time at home and may eventually become cut off from the world. Agoraphobia is not a diagnosis in itself; it is always accompanied by panic disorder.

403. (B) Compulsions are not an explicit symptom of posttraumatic stress disorder (PTSD). An individual with PTSD may have some or all of the other symptoms listed. Symptoms of PTSD include intrusive symptoms, avoidant symptoms, and symptoms of physiological arousal.

404. (B) Dissociative identity disorder, formerly known as multiple personality disorder, is characterized by distinct personalities within one person, which emerge at different times and frequently without recognition or memory of each other. This disorder is controversial and must be diagnosed only by very seasoned therapists with attention to the suggestibility of individuals who present with dissociative symptoms.

405. (A) Somatoform disorders are mental disorders, but one suffering from a somatoform disorder experiences the difficulty as physical. Therefore, somatoform disorders include physical difficulty without physical causes. Individuals suffering from a somatoform disorder may visit many doctors without getting answers about their conditions.

406. (D) Marcia likely suffers from a specific phobia, in her case, a phobia of elevators. Because of her avoidant behavior, this phobia does appear to impair her functioning in certain ways. For example, instead of choosing the best doctor for her condition, she may choose one who is accessible without an elevator.

407. (C) Obsessions are disturbing and repetitive thoughts, while compulsions are repetitive behaviors. Obsessions and compulsions are related in that compulsions are frequently a way to deal with or diminish the obsessive thoughts that one experiences.

408. (E) Phobias can be a result of classical conditioning. For example, if an individual experiences a panic attack while flying on a plane, he or she may then associate the panic with flying and develop a fear of planes. In reality, the panic may have been a result of physiological hyperarousal or have an unknown origin.

409. (B) Psychosis is known as a break from reality and is characterized by delusions (D) and hallucinations. Although psychosis is sometimes a symptom of schizophrenia (E), schizophrenia is a mental disorder and psychosis is a symptom.

410. (C) Bulimia nervosa is characterized by binge eating and compensatory behaviors. Compensatory behaviors include purging, excessive exercising, or other behaviors done after a binge to avoid weight gain.

411. (B) Dissociative disorders include dissociative fugue, dissociative amnesia, dissociative identity disorder, and depersonalization disorder. These disorders are thought to result as an adaption to very difficult circumstances during or after which an individual dissociates in order to manage the difficulty.

412. (A) Generally, the negative symptoms of schizophrenia are more difficult to identify or treat. Individuals frequently talk about and share their positive symptoms, such as delusions and hallucinations. Medications are typically designed to lessen the positive symptoms but not the negative symptoms.

413. (B) Betty is likely experiencing a somatoform disorder, or a physical ailment without a physical cause. Specifically, Betty is likely experiencing hypochondriasis. Although the experience for Betty may cause anxiety (E) and have an anxious element, the physical ailment without physical cause is the primary symptom.

414. (C) Personality disorders are thought to be pervasive and quite difficult to change. Personality disorders have a large impact on the way people interact in the world and particularly with others.

415. (A) Attention-deficit/hyperactivity disorder, or ADHD, is typically apparent in childhood but may be diagnosed in either childhood or adulthood. Key symptoms of ADHD include impulsiveness, inattention, and hyperactivity.

416. (C) This boy displays symptoms of autism. His lack of eye contact and language skills are missing developmental markers, and they speak to his difficulty in communication and socialization. Repetitive behavioral activities and sensory sensitivity are also sometimes symptoms of autism. Boys are more likely than girls to be diagnosed with autism.

417. (C) Schizophrenia does appear to have a genetic link. Identical twins are both likely to either have or not have schizophrenia, but discordant pairs of identical twins are rarely found.

418. (B) The cognitive-behavioral perspective on somatoform disorders would consider the benefits of the belief that one is sick, or the benefits one gets from behaving in certain ways. For example, one who has symptoms of hyperarousal when in public may choose to stay at home and, therefore, get many visitors and a great deal of attention due to the person's perceived illness. This is a cognitive-behavioral perspective.

419. (D) There are two different subtypes of anorexia nervosa; the restricting type is characterized by food restriction, whereas binging and purging characterize the binge-eating-purging type. Therefore, anorexia nervosa is not always characterized by binging and purging. The other choices are accurate statements about anorexia nervosa.

420. (E) The biological model of mental disorders identifies biochemical or other physiological deficiencies as the root of mental disorders. In this case, a thyroid problem is physiological and its symptoms are in part psychological.

421. (D) Paraphilias include things such as frotteurism (touching or rubbing someone in public without consent) or voyeurism (desire to watch others in sexual circumstances or in stages of undress). Paraphilias can cause problems in functioning within the mores and laws of society.

422. (C) The question describes a pattern of interacting, and it has been pervasive since childhood. Therefore, it describes Brett as suffering from a personality disorder. The specific symptoms described make it likely that Brett suffers from antisocial personality disorder.

Chapter 12: Treatment of Mental Disorders

423. (D) An internist is a physician who specializes in internal medicine or general medicine. This type of doctor may assess a patient for psychological disorders. If a patient indicates any psychological difficulty, an internist may make a referral to another type of professional to provide psychological treatment. Generally, there are many categories of professions, all with different levels and types of training, who provide psychological intervention to individuals.

424. (D) Literacy issues specifically would not cause someone to seek psychological treatment. An individual who would like to be more literate may seek a reading specialist. That said, one may seek psychological treatment in order to explore feelings related to his or her literacy. Overall, individuals do not need to have a diagnosable disorder in order to seek psychological treatment.

425. (C) Cultural competence is critical when providing psychological interventions. People from different cultures may demonstrate different symptom presentation and may respond differently to interventions. Therefore, acknowledgment and awareness of individuals from varying cultures is critical to mental health practice.

426. (B) Transference is a critical piece in psychodynamic psychotherapies. Transference is the transfer of feelings from one part of a client's life to the therapist. Many times transference is unconscious. Transference helps demonstrate a client's patterns in relationships.

427. (E) Exposure therapy is not an insight-oriented therapy. It is a behavioral therapy. Exposure therapy involves hierarchical exposure to distressing stimuli in order to reduce symptoms related to the stimuli.

428. (A) Fritz Perls founded gestalt therapy. Perls was trained as both a psychiatrist and a psychotherapist. His wife, Laura Perls, was also involved in the early days of gestalt therapy.

429. (C) Two tenets of client-centered therapy are active listening and unconditional positive regard. Active listening includes listening attentively, interacting, and demonstrating an understanding of the client. Unconditional positive regard includes maintaining a position of acceptance and lack of judgment.

430. (B) Cognitive therapy and rational emotive therapy have a focus on people's ways of thinking about themselves and about the world. Although there are some differences within these two models of therapy, the basic foundations are similar.

431. (C) A psychiatrist is a medical doctor who is trained specifically in biomedical and psychological interventions for mental disorders. Therefore, a psychiatrist may provide psychotherapy and prescribe medications for individuals with mental disorders. The other choices are professions that provide psychological interventions but do not administer biological interventions.

432. (B) Token economy is a therapy technique based on the principles of operant conditioning rather than classical conditioning. Token economy includes rewarding positive behaviors with a token-based system within which the tokens can be traded for rewards.

433. (E) Cognitive therapy was created by Aaron Beck, while Carl Rogers created client-centered therapy. Freud is known for psychoanalytic therapy.

434. (C) An individual seeking diet advice related to an iron deficiency would likely seek nutritional counseling of some sort rather than psychological treatment. There may be some psychologists or counselors who specialize in nutrition and eating, but a nutritional deficiency by itself does not warrant psychological treatment.

435. (A) A therapist who is psychoanalytically oriented, sometimes called an analyst, remains neutral when working with the client. This allows a "blank slate" from which a client can do the work.

436. (B) Exposure therapy involves gradual exposure to distressing stimuli. In Andrea's case, she will likely be exposed to the least fear-inducing circumstances first. Then she will gradually move to exposure to the most fear-inducing stimuli. The gradual exposure may allow for the client to feel that he or she can handle the fear-inducing stimuli with less discomfort than he or she had imagined.

437. (D) Psychodynamic psychotherapy does have a lens toward the unconscious and toward defenses. But it is also focused on present-day experiences and relationships. Psychodynamic psychotherapy is an outgrowth of the work of Freud and the psychoanalysts.

438. (E) No one type of psychotherapy is better than another type all of the time. The therapeutic relationship that a client and therapist build is shown to be more important than therapeutic orientation. Many therapists may practice an eclectic approach to psychotherapy, using interventions from different modalities.

439. (A) Transference is a key part of psychodynamic psychotherapy. Transference can provide data related to patterns or relationships. Countertransference (D) refers to a therapist's assignment of feelings to the client, or what the client brings up in the therapist that reminds the therapist of other parts of his or her life.

440. (B) Humanistic therapies, including client-centered therapy, have a lens toward personal strength and responsibilities. Therapists who practice in these modalities focus on positive qualities of the individuals.

441. (D) Interpersonal therapy is insight-oriented and focused on the quality of relationships that individuals have with others in their lives. The four areas of concern within the interpersonal psychotherapy model include role disputes, role transitions, interpersonal deficits, and loss.

442. (C) Flooding involves exposing someone to his or her feared or discomforting stimuli. When a person is flooded with the stimuli, it is thought that eventually that person will be able to use relaxation or coping skills to learn that he or she can deal with the fearful stimuli.

443. (C) Rational emotive therapy, originated by Albert Ellis, is founded in the belief that activating events are influenced by someone's beliefs, which then influence the consequences. This phenomenon explains why different people react much differently to the same external events.

444. (E) Cognitive therapy has proven to be an effective way to treat depression. In addition, cognitive therapy targets negative thoughts one has about oneself, circumstances, and the world at large. This particular man demonstrates these negative thinking patterns.

445. (D) Token economy is a behavioral intervention based on rewards. It is rooted in operant conditioning. Token economy involves reward for good behavior that can be exchanged for items of value to the individuals in the system.

446. (C) Gestalt therapy is focused on integrating a person's many different aspects. In this process, the entire gestalt of the person is recognized. One technique of gestalt therapy is called the "empty chair."

447. (D) Family therapists typically view the family system and its functioning as a point of intervention. Therefore, although behaviors or functioning of individuals may bring families into therapy, intervening in the entire family system is a classic family therapy approach.

448. (D) Modeling involves demonstrating other ways of behaving or thinking. In this case, the therapist demonstrates a way of thinking. Different types of modeling are present in many types of therapy, but modeling originates as behavioral intervention.

449. (B) The basis of behavioral therapies is that behavior is learned. Therefore, behavioral therapies tend to focus on unlearning old behaviors or learning new behaviors.

450. (A) Token economy involves rewarding certain behaviors. The idea behind this strategy is that the presence of the reward will increase the likelihood of the positive behavior.

451. (E) In psychoanalysis, the analyst or therapist takes a neutral stance with the client. In gestalt therapy the therapist takes a very active stance. Both of these therapies are considered insight-oriented.

452. (A) Albert Ellis is the founder of rational emotive therapy, whereas Aaron Beck is the founder of cognitive therapy. These approaches to therapy are similar and are rooted in thinking and changing maladaptive thinking.

453. (D) Systematic desensitization is considered a behavioral therapy approach. Insight-oriented therapies are focused on learning more about oneself. Behavioral approaches are also learning-based, but they are generally more cognitive and focused on changing behaviors.

454. (C) Alcoholics Anonymous is a form of self-help group. One characteristic of this group is it is member-led rather than being led by a clinician. This type of group is focused on providing mutual support to members.

455. (E) It is more common in this decade for therapists to use more than one approach in their work with patients. This may be that therapists use particular approaches for different patients, or that they use strategies and interventions from different approaches with one patient.

456. (B) A manualized treatment lends itself to clinical research because in theory all clinicians are following the same treatment guidelines, therefore providing the same treatment. For this reason manualized forms of treatment are frequently used in clinical research.

457. (B) Psychotropics is the general category of drugs used to treat mental disorders. This type of drug generally targets emotions, behaviors, or other aspects of the mind. Choices (A), (C), and (E) are types of psychotropics. Narcotics (D) are a class of drugs generally involved in pain relief. They have addictive qualities.

458. (D) A psychiatrist is a medical doctor, and medical doctors are licensed and trained to prescribe medications. All medical doctors can prescribe medications for mental disorders, but psychiatrists are trained specifically about these types of medications. In some states other professions, including nurse practitioners, have prescribing privileges.

459. (E) Antipsychotics act by blocking dopamine receptors. Dopamine is thought to be a key neurotransmitter related to psychosis and, therefore, schizophrenia. Antipsychotics appear to act only on the positive symptoms of schizophrenia and are associated with serious side effects.

460. (C) Fluoxetine, known by its brand name of Prozac, is an SSRI, or selective serotonin reuptake inhibitor. Fluoxetine is one of the first SSRIs and has been used to treat depression for many years.

461. (B) Lithium is a chemical element that is frequently used to treat bipolar disorder. Lithium does have side effects, including weight gain and dry mouth. Individuals who take lithium need to have regular blood tests, as too much lithium in the body can be quite dangerous.

462. (C) Memory loss is a common side effect of electroconvulsive therapy (ECT). Although ECT is somewhat controversial, it is still used as a treatment for various mental disorders (depression, mania, and psychosis) when other treatment regimens have been tried and found unsuccessful.

463. (B) Psychostimulants are associated with a loss of appetite. Because psychostimulants are commonly prescribed to children, nutritional intake for children on this medication must be closely monitored.

464. (B) Thorazine is a type of antipsychotic and is associated with a shuffling gate often seen in the institutionalized population, especially in the 1950s and 1960s when these medications were initially introduced. Thorazine and other antipsychotics are used less frequently since the introduction of atypical antipsychotics (C) because these medications have fewer side effects and do act on negative symptoms.

465. (C) Rather than stimulating the nervous system, benzodiazepines act by sedating, or slowing down, the nervous system. The other choices are true of benzodiazepines.

466. (C) Bipolar disorder is characterized by depressed mood states and manic or hypomanic mood states. Therefore, a mood stabilizer is often used to treat bipolar disorder. Atypical antipsychotics are also sometimes used to treat bipolar disorder, but traditional antipsychotics (A) are not.

467. (A) A prefrontal lobotomy, a type of psychosurgery, is a brain surgery procedure originally aimed at decreasing the pathology in an individual. After many prefrontal lobotomies were performed, the initial positive results gave way to very negative side effects. Although other psychosurgeries may reemerge in the future, this particular technique is rarely, if ever, used today.

468. (D) Psychostimulants are commonly used to treat ADHD and include medications such as Ritalin and Adderall.

469. (B) Atypical antipsychotic medications are known to target both positive and negative symptoms of schizophrenia. Previously developed antipsychotic medications act only on the positive symptoms of schizophrenia. Although the side effects of atypical antipsychotics are different from other antipsychotics, there are still known side effects.

470. (C) Deinstitutionalization occurred after the development of antipsychotic medication. The process began in the 1950s in the United States. The ability of community-based treatment to support former institutionalized individuals has been under scrutiny.

471. (D) MAOIs, TCAs, SSRIs, and SNRIs are examples of antidepressants. The more commonly used antidepressants at this point are SSRIs and SNRIs, but the others are sometimes used.

472. (B) Electroconvulsive therapy is used to treat severe depression that is considered treatment resistant. For example, an individual with severe depression who has been on many different types of medications and has been actively involved in psychotherapy with no results, may benefit from electroconvulsive therapy. The other choices do not describe biomedical interventions.

473. (E) Anxiolytics are typically used to treat anxiety. Panic attacks are a manifestation of extreme anxiety, and panic disorder is a type of anxiety disorder.

474. (C) Bipolar disorder and schizophrenia are both sometimes associated with psychosis and, therefore, are treated with atypical antipsychotics. Mood stabilizers (D) are associated with the treatment of bipolar disorder but not schizophrenia, and SSRIs (A) can sometimes be harmful to those with bipolar disorder.

Chapter 13: Research

475. (B) A randomized control consists of more than one intervention. For example, a study may be designed where one group receives psychotherapy and one receives medications. Participants are randomly assigned to a group, thus the name *randomized controlled trial*.

476. (A) The Beck Depression Index is a well-researched tool to assess depression. Scores on the Beck Depression Index could operationalize depression for a study. The number of times someone cries may not be a valid way to operationalize depression, as someone may cry for reasons other than depression (e.g., happiness). The other choices do not address levels of depression, rather just presence of depression.

477. (D) A sample is drawn from a population, which is a larger group with the characteristics that fit study criteria. Cases (A) and individual subjects (B) may be part of a sample, but a sample is drawn from a population.

478. (A) Play therapy is the independent variable. An independent variable is the variable that is being examined to see if it has an impact on the dependent variable.

479. (B) Reliability refers to the consistency of a test. In order for it to be reliable, a test that measures a particular quality of a group of individuals should yield similar results, even if the order of questions is changed.

480. (A) The fact that survey methods rely on self-report data is a limitation rather than advantage of this type of methodology. Self-report data are not observable, and subjects may present biased information in their responses.

481. (D) The variables in this example both go in the same direction, in that more exercise is related to higher quality of life scores. Because the variables move in the same direction, they are considered positively correlated. To find the correlation coefficient, a statistical equation is used.

482. (B) Naturalistic observation involves observing behaviors or interactions in the community with no researcher involvement or intervention. A limitation to this approach is the presence of the researcher. For example, although a researcher observing children would not interact with the children, the fact there is an adult researcher in the environment may alter behaviors.

483. (C) The dependent variable is the response to the intervention. The intervention is the independent variable.

484. (B) In random sampling, all members of the population have an equal chance of being chosen for the study.

485. (B) The psychoeducation group is the independent variable. This study would seek to explore if participation in this type of group plays a factor in alcohol use.

486. (E) Validity describes the extent an assessment tool or other procedure measures what it claims to or intends to measure.

487. (D) Experimenter bias occurs when the researcher or a member of the research team interprets results in order to support the hypothesis or the expected outcomes. The experimenter may not do this consciously, but it may occur as a subconscious process. The possibility of experimenter bias must be considered when designing studies.

488. (C) Psychological phenomena overall is a broad subject, and describing all psychological phenomena is a large, insurmountable task. All other choices do describe purposes of psychological research.

489. (C) The population in this question is the 1,000 adults more than 50 years old in this town. Each of the adults has a 25 percent chance of being chosen for the study. Because all members of the population have an equal chance of being chosen, it is considered random sampling.

490. (A) An experimental design helps to establish cause-and-effect relationships. Experimental designs include independent and dependent variables. The impact of a certain psychological treatment versus no treatment on a population of individuals with schizophrenia could be explored using an experimental design.

491. (C) Informed consent is critical to all human subject research. Informed consent gives potential participants all of the relevant information about their participation and allows potential participants to opt out of participating. Informed consent is sometimes a signed form, and other times it is implied.

492. (D) To remain ethically sound, a study must allow participants to withdraw if they feel the need or the desire to do so. Although this withdrawal will impact study outcomes, participants should not feel coerced into participation in the study at any point along the way.

493. (A) The method of concealing the study purpose is called deception. The use of deception is at times considered ethical if there is no other way to collect data and the deception will not cause harm to participants. There are some documented past research studies that involved deception and were harmful to participants.

494. (C) Institutional review boards (IRBs) are established at all universities that engage in human subjects research. These boards are responsible for reviewing research for ethical considerations. They may request that researchers make changes to the research methodology for ethical reasons.

495. (B) Informed consent is a critical process in psychology research, but informed consent can be gathered in different ways. Signed forms and implied consent by participation are two ways of getting informed consent.

496. (C) Human subject researchers are expected to do no harm. Human subject research seeks to explore various human experiences but not at a harmful cost to participants. During the Stanford Prison Experiment, the different levels of power given to the participants with little guidelines or intervention led to participant harm.

497. (D) Deception is a technique used to conceal the purpose of the research. At times researchers give participants a false purpose in order to prevent participant bias. This technique is ethically controversial and must be reviewed in depth if it is to be used.

498. (D) Confidentiality is an important ethical principle in psychology research. Confidentiality is the principle of maintaining subjects' privacy. Protecting confidentiality ensures that information gleaned by the research project is not identified to a particular participant by anyone other than the researcher. The subject's participation in the research itself is also kept confidential by the researchers in ethical research. Confidentiality is a key principle in other psychology practices, including psychotherapy and psychological testing.

499. (C) A debriefing is sometimes used to provide more information to a participant and to ensure that the research did not cause harm. Sometimes debriefing is used if the research design involves deception. In this case, subjects would be told the true purpose of the research and allowed to respond. Referrals are made during debriefings if participants had an emotional response to being in the research and would like further support around this.

500. (B) This study involved deception. Although participants volunteered for the study, the purpose of the study was concealed. Additionally, the participants were deceived as to the amount of shock they were giving to others because those receiving shock were not actually receiving shock but were acting. Researchers in this case believed they could not get appropriate results if participants were made fully aware of the purpose of the study. The use of deception has numerous ethical considerations.

ς